Rigor in the Remote Learning Classroom

Learn how to keep the rigor and motivation alive in a remote learning or hybrid K–12 classroom. In this essential book, bestselling author Barbara R. Blackburn shares frameworks and tools to help you move online without compromising the rigor of your instruction. You'll learn . . .

- ◆ how to create a remote culture of high expectations;
- ◆ how to scaffold so students reach higher levels of learning;
- ◆ how to have students collaborate in different settings; and
- ◆ how to provide virtual feedback and deliver effective assessments.

You'll also discover how common activities, such as virtual field trips, can lack rigor without critical thinking prompts. The book provides practical strategies you can implement immediately to help all students reach higher levels of success.

Barbara R. Blackburn is the bestselling author of over 25 books and is a sought-after consultant. She was an award-winning professor at Winthrop University and has taught students of all ages. Barbara can be contacted through her website at www.barbarablackburnonline.com.

Melissa Miles is a middle school language arts teacher. Previously, she was Director of Educational Resources at a school in North Carolina. She has almost 20 years of classroom teaching experience. She is also twice credentialed as a National Board-Certified teacher, works as a SpringBoard Curriculum consultant to College Board, and is a certified member of the site visitation team for the Schools to Watch award.

Rigor in the Remote Learning Classroom

Instructional Tips and Strategies

Barbara R. Blackburn with Melissa Miles

Routledge
Taylor & Francis Group

NEW YORK AND LONDON

First published 2021
by Routledge
52 Vanderbilt Avenue, New York, NY 10017

and by Routledge
2 Park Square, Milton Park, Abingdon, Oxon, OX14 4RN

Routledge is an imprint of the Taylor & Francis Group, an informa business

Library of Congress Cataloging-in-Publication Data
Names: Blackburn, Barbara R., 1961– author.
Title: Rigor in the remote learning classroom : instructional tips and strategies / Barbara R. Blackburn.
Description: New York, NY : Routledge, 2021. | Includes bibliographical references.
Identifiers: LCCN 2020027914 (print) | LCCN 2020027915 (ebook) | ISBN 9780367620103 (paperback) | ISBN 9780367615468 (hardback) | ISBN 9781003107484 (ebook)
Subjects: LCSH: Web-based instruction. | Effective teaching. | Motivation in education. | Academic achievement. | Educational tests and measurements.
Classification: LCC LB1044.87 .B59 2021 (print) | LCC LB1044.87 (ebook) | DDC 371.33/44678—dc23
LC record available at https://lccn.loc.gov/2020027914
LC ebook record available at https://lccn.loc.gov/2020027915

ISBN: 978-0-367-61546-8 (hbk)
ISBN: 978-0-367-62010-3 (pbk)
ISBN: 978-1-003-10748-4 (ebk)

Typeset in Palatino
by Apex CoVantage, LLC

I dedicate this book to Melissa (Missy) Miles, one of my former graduate students, a consultant for my professional development company, a twice-certified National Board Certified Teacher, parent, and my friend. I admire her for her passion for teaching and her students, her dedication to her students, her skillful strategies for technology instruction, and her love of her children. I also appreciate how she has combined all of the above to provide quality professional development for teachers.

Contents

Meet the Authors

Barbara R. Blackburn, named a Top 30 Global Guru in Education, has dedicated her life to raising the level of rigor and motivation for professional educators and students alike. What differentiates Barbara's over 25 books are her easily executable concrete examples based on decades of experience as a teacher, professor and consultant. Barbara's dedication to education was inspired in her early years by her parents. Her father's doctorate and lifetime career as a professor taught her the importance of professional training. Her mother's career as a school secretary shaped Barbara's appreciation of the effort all staff play in the education of every student. Barbara has taught early childhood, elementary, middle and high school students and has served as an educational consultant for three publishing companies. She holds a master's degree in school administration and was certified as a teacher and school principal in North Carolina. She received her PhD in Curriculum and Teaching from the University of North Carolina at Greensboro. In 2006, she received the award for Outstanding Junior Professor at Winthrop University. She left her position at the University of North Carolina at Charlotte to write and speak full time.

In addition to speaking at state, national and international conferences, she regularly presents workshops for teachers and administrators in elementary, middle and high schools. Her workshops are lively and engaging and filled with practical information. Her most popular seminars include:

- ◆ Rigor Is NOT a Four-Letter Word
- ◆ Rigorous Schools and Classrooms: Leading the Way
- ◆ Rigorous Assessments
- ◆ Differentiating Instruction Without Lessening Rigor in Your Classroom
- ◆ Motivation + Engagement + Rigor = Student Success

- ◆ Rigor for Students With Special Needs
- ◆ Motivating Struggling Students
- ◆ Rigor in the Remote Learning Classroom

Barbara can be reached through her website: www.barbara blackburnonline.com.

Melissa Miles is currently back in the classroom teaching middle school language arts after serving as Director of Educational Resources at a school in Charlotte, North Carolina. She has almost 20 years of classroom teaching experience. She is also twice credentialed as a National Board-Certified teacher for young adolescents, works as a SpringBoard Curriculum consultant to College Board, and is a certified member of the site visitation team for the Schools to Watch award. She is coauthor of *Rigor in the 6–12 ELA and Social Studies Classroom* and *Rigor in the K–5 ELA and Social Studies Classroom* with Barbara Blackburn.

Preface

The COVID-19 pandemic changed schooling around the world. Many times with little notice, teachers were expected to teach remotely. Technology tools were varied, and oftentimes, there was no teacher training, which complicated matters. Issues such as student access to computers; lack of internet or Wi-Fi hotspots; and students' physical, emotional and social needs, including nutritious meals, complicated a focus on instruction.

When I spoke with teachers, I heard an additional concern: "My school is working on equity issues, and I know how to use technology. But I find myself lowering the level of rigor in my instruction to make up for the technical complications of remote learning." This book addresses that issue. It is not a basic "How to Use Technology" or a "Solving Equity Issues in Online Learning" book. If those are your needs (and they are certainly valid ones), there are other resources available. In this book, I am focused specifically on a different instructional issue: how to ensure and increase rigor in your remote learning classroom.

Throughout the book, you will find practical strategies that can be used in an on-site or remote classroom. However, you'll also see that specific remote learning recommendations are integrated with the strategies. I tend to provide examples of various technology tools, rather than asking you to be dependent on one platform. I also try to give you free options in addition to paid ones. As always, you'll want to pick the one(s) that best meet the needs of your students.

In Chapter 1, we will discuss the myths related to rigor and the definition for rigor, as well as key aspects of remote learning. In Chapter 2, we'll focus on the planning aspects of rigorous remote learning. Chapters 3 and 5 are companions covering how to increase expectations and how to demonstrate learning that meets those expectations. You may choose to read these together.

In Chapter 4, we'll emphasize the support and scaffolding needed to aid students so they can be successful with rigorous remote work. This is a critical aspect of rigor, and one you want to pay particular attention to. Chapter 6 details aspects of both formative and summative assessment, with specific examples and suggestions for remote learning strategies. Finally, in Chapter 7, we'll look at several challenges you are likely facing: student motivation, creating a positive remote climate and working with parents and families.

It is my goal for you to immediately use what you read in this book. Each chapter is organized into smaller topics. At the end of Chapters 2 through 7, you'll find *Points to Ponder*, which will allow you to reflect on your learning. Finally, you can contact me through my website, www.barbarablackburnonline. com. I would like to hear from you as you implement the ideas from the book. One of the best parts of writing a book occurs when teachers and students share how they took an idea and made it their own. As you read the chapters, I hope you will find ideas that will enhance your classroom. Enjoy the journey to new learning!

Acknowledgments

To my father and co-author of *Advocacy from A to Z*, who died on Thanksgiving 2019. He has always been my role model, and this is the first book he did not read. I miss him.

To my stepson, Hunter, who died on March 21, 2020, at the age of 22. There are not enough words to describe how I feel. He has always provided a student perspective as I wrote.

To my husband, Pete, who is always my mainstay, inspiration and continuous encourager.

To my best friend, Abbigail Armstrong, who provides a listening ear and critical feedback that makes me better.

To my mother, sisters and brothers-in-law, who provide support and encouragement.

To my editor and publisher, Lauren Davis, who is simply the best. She provides me opportunities to share my passion and knowledge, and, together, we produce books that are far better than I could do alone.

To Autumn Spalding, who is hands down the best project manager I have ever worked with.

To Emma Capel, who always designs a creative cover.

To Apex CoVantage, which takes care of the nuts and bolts of production.

1

Rigor and Remote Learning

Remote learning has increased in popularity with schools. As we talk about instruction in the remote classroom, we tend to discuss the logistics or tools that will help us teach. Sometimes, focusing on ensuring rigor is forgotten. Another issue is that everyone seems to have a different understanding of what rigor means, especially what it looks like in the remote learning classroom. In this chapter, we'll look at the myths and realities related to rigor, as well as vocabulary and beliefs of remote learning. As a baseline, when I discuss remote learning, I am talking about any learning in which the teacher and student are in a setting that is not traditional.

Myths About Rigor

First, let's look at misconceptions about the concept of rigor. There are ten commonly held beliefs about rigor that are not true.

Ten Myths About Rigor

Myth 1: Lots of homework is a sign of rigor.

Myth 2: Rigor means doing more.

Myth 3: Rigor is not for struggling students or those with special needs.

Myth 4: When you increase rigor, student motivation decreases.

Myth 5: Providing support means lessening rigor.

Myth 6: Resources equal rigor.

Myth 7: Standards alone take care of rigor.

Myth 8: Rigor means you have to quit doing everything you do now and start over.

Myth 9: Rigor is just one more thing to do.

Myth 10: Rigor is not for early childhood or primary students.

As you think about your current instruction in a remote learning environment, consider each of those myths. Which are most common during remote learning? Each of these is a popular myth, but there are several that are not specific, but particularly applicable to remote learning. I find that Myth 2 about doing more is quite common when teaching remotely. With pressure to feel like we are doing "real teaching," we sometimes give more work, rather than focusing on quality. I also find that Myth 6 about resources is a typical belief related to remote learning. Your school or district may have purchased a program, and we simply assume it is rigorous. That may or may not be true. Finally, Myths 3 and 5 are especially applicable for remote learning. Students who struggle, whether they are students with special needs, English learners or any other student who needs extra help, are capable of rigorous work. They simply need additional scaffolding, strategies that will support learning in a remote setting.

What Is Rigor?

You may have heard some of those myths about rigor. But when we delve into what rigor really means, it is focused on student learning.

"Rigor is creating an environment in which each student is expected to learn at high levels; each student is supported so he or she can learn at high levels; and each student demonstrates learning at high levels."

(Blackburn, 2018)

Notice we are looking at the environment you create. The trifold approach to rigor is not limited to the curriculum that students are expected to learn. It is more than a specific lesson or instructional strategy. It is deeper than what a student says or does in response to a lesson. True rigor is the result of weaving together all elements of schooling to raise students to higher levels of learning. We will look at a brief description of each of the core areas in what follows, but we will explore each area in more depth, providing specific activities and strategies, in upcoming chapters.

Expectations

The first component of rigor is creating an environment in which each student is expected to learn at high levels. Having high expectations starts with the recognition that every student possesses the potential to succeed at his or her individual level. Almost every teacher or leader I talk with says, "We have high expectations for our students." Sometimes that is evidenced by the behaviors in the school; other times, however, faculty actions don't match the words. There are concrete ways to implement and assess rigor in classrooms. As you design lessons that incorporate more rigorous opportunities for learning, you will want to consider the questions that are embedded in the instruction. Higher-level questioning is an integral part of a rigorous classroom. Look for open-ended questions, ones that are at higher levels of critical thinking. It is also important to pay attention to how you respond to student questions. When I visit schools, it is not uncommon to see teachers who ask higher-level questions. But for whatever reason, I then see some of the same teachers accept low-level responses from students. In rigorous class-rooms, teachers push students to respond at high levels. They ask extending questions. Extending questions are questions that encourage a student to explain their reasoning and think through ideas. When a student does not know the immediate answer but has sufficient background information to provide a response to the question, the teacher continues to probe and guide the student's thinking rather than moving on to the next student. Insist on thinking past the concrete, literal answer.

As you can see, by probing further and expecting more complex responses from students, whether in a video session or through written questions in a chat, teachers can assist them in gaining deeper meaning and making more thorough connections. The first answer students give is oftentimes quite concrete and literal, but if you consistently push them to peel back layers and apply higher-level thought processes, they will eventually realize you expect high-level thinking and begin doing it naturally. This will increase the level of rigor in your classroom. We'll explore expectations in a remote classroom in more depth in Chapter 3.

Scaffolding for Support

High expectations are important, but rigorous remote learning classrooms assure that each student is supported so he or she can learn at high levels, which is the second part of our definition. It is essential that teachers design lessons that move students to more challenging work while simultaneously providing ongoing scaffolding to support students' learning as they move to those higher levels.

Providing additional scaffolding throughout lessons is one of the most important ways to support your students. Oftentimes students have the ability or knowledge to accomplish a task but are overwhelmed by the complexity of it, therefore getting lost in the process. This can occur in a variety of ways, but it requires that teachers ask themselves during every step of their lessons, "What extra support might my students need?" It is up to the teacher, as practitioner, to anticipate where students may hit roadblocks and to react in the moment in providing additional stair steps for students as needed.

Examples of Scaffolding Strategies

♦ Asking/using guiding questions during a video presentation or in written form for independent learning.

♦ Preteaching vocabulary with independent materials prior to a video presentation.

♦ Providing graphic organizers to help students process text.

♦ Highlighting or color-coding steps in a project.

♦ Modeling with think-alouds with a recorded video.

♦ Accessing prior knowledge or providing prior knowledge through a virtual tour.

♦ Employing an "I do—we do—you do" approach as a gradual release of responsibility.

If a particular standard requires second-grade students to understand the water cycle but a student has difficulty accessing the grade-level text, perhaps the teacher can offer a short biographical/documentary video to build background knowledge and then diffuse the difficult vocabulary in the text or provide guiding questions that naturally chunk the text. These scaffolding strategies will allow that student to reach the same end goal, which is mastery of the standard.

Similarly, if a student with special needs struggles with writing, but standards require skills in narrating a story, a teacher might first break down the elements by allowing the student to draw the sequence of events using Sketchboard then tell the story verbally in his or her own words using the picture sequence and finally attempt to write the story on paper. Afterward, the students may need to read a mentor text and circle the descriptive details that enhance the story, use a graphic organizer to brainstorm descriptive details to include in his or her own story and finally add in the details that seem to fit well. These activities would be the "in-between" steps to help the student achieve the standard of being able to use sequencing and descriptive details to tell a story. Chapter 4 will provide a range of scaffolding strategies you can use with any grade level and content area.

Demonstration of Learning

The third component of a rigorous classroom is providing each student with opportunities to demonstrate learning at high levels. There are two aspects of students' demonstration of learning. First, we need to provide rigorous tasks and assignments for students. What we've learned is that if we want students to show they understand what they learned at a high level, we also need to provide opportunities for students to demonstrate they have truly mastered that learning at more than a basic level. Many teachers use Bloom's Taxonomy or Webb's Depth of Knowledge (DOK; Level 3 or above is rigorous). I prefer Webb's DOK for a more accurate view of the depth and complexity of rigor, and we'll explain that more fully in Chapter 3.

Examples of Guidelines for Rigor for *Bloom's Taxonomy and Webb's Depth of Knowledge (DOK)*	
Bloom's Taxonomy	*Webb's DOK Level 3*
Analyzing	Does the assessment focus on deeper knowledge?
Evaluating	Are students proposing and evaluating solutions or recognizing and explaining misconceptions?
Creating	Do students go beyond the text information while demonstrating they understand the text?
	Do students support their ideas with evidence?
**Please note that although the verbs are important, you must pay attention to what comes after the verb to determine if it is rigorous.	Does the assessment require reasoning, planning, using evidence and a higher level of thinking than the previous two levels (such as a deeper level of inferencing)?

Second, in order for students to demonstrate their learning, each one must be engaged in academic tasks. In too many classrooms, most of the instruction consists of teacher-centered, large-group instruction, perhaps in an interactive lecture or discussion format. The general practice during these lessons is for the teacher to ask a question and then call on a student to respond. While this provides an opportunity for one student to demonstrate understanding, the remaining students don't do so. Another option would be for the teacher to allow all students to think–pair–share, respond electronically with a thumbs up or down, post answers in a chat or on a shared document, or answer polls that tally the responses. Such activities hold each student accountable for demonstrating his or her understanding. You'll find information, including sample tasks and assessments, in Chapters 3, 5 and 6.

Remote Learning

Now, let's turn our attention to remote learning. First, there are key terms related to remote learning that provide a common base for understanding.

Terms Related to Remote Learning

Asynchronous Learning Students access information and learn at various times. Typically, the teacher provides independent work, which may happen individually or in small groups.

Synchronous Learning Students are learning at the same time, which allows for real-time interaction with the teacher. Video presentations are the most typical example of synchronous learning.

Gamification Instruction based on gaming principles, including the use of point scoring, trophies and badges; various "levels"; and leaderboards to increase engagement.

Hybrid Learning Sometimes called blended learning, this is a mix of in-person and online or remote learning.

Learning Management System (LMS) A software program where instruction and assessment are available. Typically, students are assessed, and instruction is provided based on that assessment.

Social Media Learning: Social media learning refers to building of student learning through collaboration, discussion and creation and sharing of content through platforms such as blogs, wikis, Twitter and Facebook.

Virtual Classroom: Virtual classrooms take place over the internet rather than in a physical classroom.

Next, it's important to consider beliefs about rigor and remote learning. Based on my decades of experience in education and my years of experience teaching remotely, I have found there are eight core beliefs to support student learning in a remote setting.

Both the remainder of this book and blending rigor with remote learning as a whole, are based on these beliefs. You'll see that I provided specific chapters that address each belief within the box.

Core Beliefs About Rigor and Remote Learning

1. Remote learning uses best practices in instruction but adapts them to a virtual setting (entire book).
2. Remote learning should provide opportunities for student engagement, although it may look different from the physical classroom (entire book).
3. Blending synchronous and asynchronous learning will likely be the best way to support your instruction (entire book).
4. Planning ensures you can accomplish your goals with rigorous remote learning (Chapter 2).
5. Expectations for learning should be high in terms of content, not just technology or creativity (Chapters 3 and 5).
6. Scaffolding and support are key to student success. Scaffolding may occur with the whole class, small groups or individuals (Chapter 4).
7. Allowing for different assessment options, including an emphasis on performance-based assessment, is important, since traditional assessment methods may not be as effective in a remote learning setting (Chapter 6).
8. Partnering with parents and families is critical to ensure student success (Chapter 7).

A Final Note

There are many times that we are so focused on the logistics of remote learning that we forget about instructional rigor. However, once we understand what rigor is (and is not), as well as basic terminology and beliefs about remote learning, we discover that rigor enhances remote learning in ways that encourage student success.

2

Planning for Rigorous Learning in the Remote Classroom

Before we look at instructional aspects of rigor in a remote learning classroom, let's start with planning. Although planning is an essential part of any instruction, I find it to be even more so with remote learning, since we need to consider the tool(s) that will help us accomplish our goals. In this chapter, we'll look at four broad areas related to planning.

> A General Planning Model
> Technology-Specific Planning
> Considerations When Planning Lessons
> Integrating Questioning Into Lessons

A General Planning Model

There are a variety of ways to plan. When I was a first-year teacher, I simply looked through my resources, planned my lesson and matched it to an objective. Then I wrote or adapted a test or project to measure what my students learned. Now, I realize that wasn't the most effective option. However, that process is still used in some classrooms for planning instruction and assessment, but this doesn't necessarily ensure rigor.

An alternative I prefer is the Task Cycle. I researched this model from the DuPont Corporation while working on my doctorate. The Task Cycle focuses on starting with the rationale (or purpose) and desired result (product) before determining the process or resources needed.

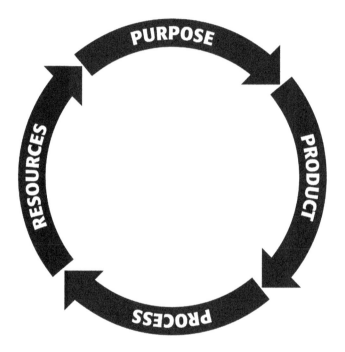

This is particularly helpful with remote learning. Too often, we start with the process (how to get there given online or remote platforms) and resources (what we use to teach). For example, perhaps what I plan is for students to learn about Martin Luther King Jr. and the Civil Rights Movement by viewing (process) his "I Have a Dream" speech online (resource).

Let's turn that around with the Task Cycle. The purpose is that we want students to understand the impact Martin Luther King Jr. had on the Civil Rights Movement (purpose) and we want them to demonstrate their understanding through a podcast (product). To do that, students will need to read about Martin Luther King Jr. and watch the "I Have a Dream" speech (process) using online news articles and the video (resources).

By starting with our purpose and product, which is the assessment, we can ensure a higher-quality, more rigorous lesson. As we move forward in our discussion of the Task Cycle, we will be focusing on planning and its impact on instruction, scaffolding and assessment.

Purpose

The first part of the Task Cycle is to decide on the purpose. The purpose will be embedded throughout all parts of the cycle. As you determine your purpose, make sure that you start with rigorous goals, standards, objectives and learning targets. Generally, with the national push for more rigorous standards, we have seen increased challenge and complexity in state and national standards. However, I've seen instances of teachers simplifying those standards, and in the process, watering down the rigor.

How can you ensure that you are truly meeting your standards, objectives, and goals? First, look beyond the verbs in the standard. The verb only tells part of the story. A verb like "apply" can mean a basic application or an application at a high level, depending on the context of the standard. For example, I can apply what I learned by drawing a picture that summarizes the story or apply what I learned by designing a solution to the climate change crisis. You can also measure your objectives and learning targets against a standard measure of rigor, such as Webb's Depth of Knowledge.

Product

After you have determined your purpose, then you decide on the product. Since there are a variety of assessments to choose from, you'll want to make sure you plan the best type to match your purpose. There are three general principles for choosing or developing a rigorous assessment as your product.

General Principles

Match the type of assessment to the purpose.
Incorporate rigor throughout the product.
Stay on track.

First, match the type of assessment you want to use with the purpose of the assessment. For example, if you want students to demonstrate knowledge of facts, the best assessment may be a multiple-choice question or a short-answer question that requires a list response. But if you want students to demonstrate problem-solving skills as well as an understanding of cross-pollination, a performance-based assessment, such as the design and completion of an experiment, is appropriate.

You'll also want to consider the learning format. For example, do you want students to create an electronic portfolio (and do they have that capability)? Or perhaps a conversation in a format such as chat or Reddit? In a remote learning setting, this is a critical consideration as you determine your assessments.

Next, incorporate rigor throughout the assessment. As we explore the different types of assessment throughout the book, I'll include specific recommendations for rigor for each type. For now, generally, you should:

- ◆ include a focus on higher-order thinking skills;
- ◆ include problem-solving;
- ◆ include justifications and explanations in responses.

Finally, be sure you don't get off track. Recently, I was assessing samples of student assignments in elementary, middle and high schools. One consistent theme I discovered was that many assessments were very creative, but the academic work was not rigorous, nor did they match the goals, standards, objectives or learning targets. I believe in creative, engaging activities, but if the assessment is focused on that, you can miss the academic piece. For the samples I evaluated, students spent the majority of their time on the artistic, creative side of the assignment, whether it was creating a video or a Prezi. The assessments provided evidence of students' creativity, but less about their understanding of content. It's particularly important to balance the two.

I would also add that staying on track includes remote learning considerations. There are times when it is easy to veer off into the latest technology or get caught up in using too many different tools. Variety is fine, but don't overwhelm your students.

Process

In the process part of the cycle, you work backward from your product. Now that you know where you want to end up, you determine how to accomplish your goals. Planning how you teach a lesson is where your creativity can thrive! Think of ways you can engage your students in remote learning, knowing that practicality in terms of your tools and/or platforms will be a major consideration.

Resources

The final part of the Task Cycle to consider is the resources needed. What resources will you need for your lesson or project? Consider all resources, whether it is a specific text or website students need to access, or the technology tool students will use, such as group chats for projects.

Sample Learning Tools

Novare PBL Platform is a project management tool that uses narratives, portfolios and learning goals to structure project-based learning.

SeeSaw provides tools for all learners (especially younger ones) to take pictures and drawings and create videos to demonstrate learning.

Prezi incorporates video, audio and other interactive research components for a presentation that keeps everyone's attention.

Project Foundry is a popular learning tool that enables students to plan their own learning and track their progress. It also makes organizing student projects much easier for students and teachers. Schools also love that Project Foundry gives students the chance to build digital portfolios—a necessary skill in today's evolving technological culture.

JamBoard allows teachers to create lesson plan boards; students can also create and share from different locations.

Kami is a PDF document annotator with multiple options for students to respond; it also links to multiple other platforms such as Canvas, Schoology and Google Classroom.

Scribble Press allows students options to share the work that they've done with others while reflecting on the experience as a whole. Scribble Press allows students to write and illustrate their own books, as well as retell the story of their challenge-based experience, include final project results and reflect on moments of personal growth.

Blank Task Cycle Template	
Purpose	
Standard	
Objectives	
Learning Goals	
Process	
Products	
Resources	

Technology-Specific Planning

Personal Digital Inquiry

Personal Digital Inquiry (Coiro, Dobler, & Pelekis, 2019) is a way of teaching and planning that incorporates exploration, collaboration, discussion, application, analysis and reflection. It is designed to challenge students to both build and express knowledge, as well as take action based on their learning.

There are four stages in Personal Digital Inquiry. Although I have organized them in a chart, the designers used a circular graphic. For each of the four stages, here, I've provided technology tools that may be useful.

Wonder and Discover	Collaborate and Discuss	Create and Take Action	Analyze and Reflect
Spiderscribe NearPod BrainPop DiscoveryEd KidsDiscover CNN10 TweenTribune TeenTribune Factmonster Newsround	Kami NowComment Google Docs YoTeach Kialo Flipgrid Diigo Mindmeister SeeSaw Voicethread Padlet Lino	Kami NearPod Glogster Animoto JamBoard Kialo ThingLink Whiteboard.fi Creaza ExplainEverything AdobeSpark	Kami eduBlogs Flipgrid SeeSaw JamBoard Educreation Voicethread Padlet Lino AnswerGarden

Learning Innovation Catalyst

The Learning Innovation Catalyst (see pp. 19–20) provides a six-part design for continued distance learning. Components include Establishing Communication Structures, Setting Clear Expectations, Getting Ready, Planning for Access, Establishing Community Connections and Social Emotional Care.

Although the template provided on pages 19 and 20 is designed for school districts, it is easy to adapt to your own classroom. For example, even though Getting Ready focuses on professional development, you will want to consider what you need in terms of knowledge, resources and other support so you will be successful.

Learning Innovation Catalyst

My School's Plan for Continued Distance Learning

School Name: **District Non-Negotiables**

Principal:
Principal Phone:
Principal Email:

Secondary Contact:
Secondary Contact Phone:
Secondary Contact Email:

Priority	How
1. Establish Communication Structures and Protocols	Frequency of Check-ins for: • Teachers: _____ • Students: _____ • Families: _____ School/District Landing Page: Person(s) Responsible for Responding to Parent and Community Questions: District Administration
2. Set Clear Expectations for Remote Structures and Routines	Our Remote School Day Schedule • Start Time: _____ • End Time: _____ • Breaks: _____ How Teachers will be present: How Students will be present: How Families will be included and supported: Other Expectations and Routines: Teachers will collaborate with intervention specialists.
3. Get Your Teachers and Distance Learning Toolkit Ready!	When and how initial PD will happen: When and how ongoing PD will happen: Resources for PD: Digital Tools and Other Resources (list primary tools): How Our Students Will Access Learning: Online learning, pencil/paper packets Technology that will be available for students:

4. Plan for Access to Technology and Your Digital Toolkit	Technology that will be available for Teachers:
	How Teachers will access technology and other resources:
	Plan for Onboarding Students into Digital Tools and Resources:
	Communication Plan for Parents:
	Intervention Support Plan:
5. Establish Community Connections	Community Locations and Resources that will be available for Students and Families:
6. Take care of your community - Social and Emotional Care	How we will connect with community:
	Supports for Social and Emotional Learning Needs:
	Plan to help foster connection of students to teachers and peers:
	Plan for Students who may need extra support:

Considerations When Planning Lessons

You'll also find that certain students will struggle with various issues, such as not feeling connected to the teacher or not feeling successful. There are specific strategies to address key issues.

For learners who struggle with . . .	Do this . . .
Seeing relevance	Develop real-life learning experiences and applications.
Not enjoying the activity	Attempt to involve the student more in the activity or provide an alternative activity.
Poor relationships with peers	Use care when assigning groups, design activities that build collaboration and pair students with a "coach" to help them assimilate into group work.
Poor relationships with teachers	Take time to build a more positive relationship with the student. Take it as your responsibility to improve the relationship. Check in with an individual student via either technology or a phone call.
Not feeling successful	Provide small chunks of tasks that students can complete successfully. Reinforce the successes. Provide weekly and daily schedules. Number assignments to help students track progress.
Thinking they are not successful when they are	Show them why they are successful. Positively reinforce the effort and achievement.
Thinking they are successful when they are not	Reinforce that they have tried, but point out where they have made mistakes and provide coaching and support to help them succeed.
Struggling with reading text online	Teach students how reading online is different from reading traditional text, as well as teach them to ignore distractions (ads, links).

Questioning as a Part of Planning

A final part of planning is the use of questioning. Asking questions is a standard part of any teacher's repertoire. However, the type of questions you ask makes a difference. In this section, we'll look at seven aspects of questioning.

Seven Aspects of Questioning

Strengths and Weaknesses of Questioning
Habits of Effective Questioners
FIRE Questions
Three Classifications
Teaching Students to Ask Questions
Question Stems or Starters
Asking and Answering a Question

Strengths and Weaknesses of Questioning

Terry Heick of TeachThought describes the difference between the relative strengths and weaknesses of questions.

THE RELATIVE STRENGTHS OF QUESTIONS	THE RELATIVE WEAKNESSES OF QUESTIONS
Questions fit in well with the modern "Google" mindset	Questions can imply answers, which imply stopping points and "finishing" over inquiry and wisdom
Questions promote inquiry and learning how to learn over proving what you know	Accuracy of answers can be overvalued, which makes the confidence of the answerer impact the quality of the response significantly
Good questions can reveal subtle shades of understanding–what this student knows about this topic in this context	"Bad questions" are easy to write and deeply confusing, which can accumulate to harm a student's sense of self-efficacy, as well as their own tendency to ask them on their own
Used well, questions can promote personalized learning as teachers can change question on fly to meet student needs	Questions depend on language, which means literacy, jargon, confusing syntax, academic diction, and more can all obscure the learning process

www.teachthought.com/critical-thinking/quick-guide-questioning-classroom/

Habits of Effective Questioners

Next, James Cooper (2006), in his book *Classroom Teaching Skills*, helps us understand how we can effectively use questioning with our students. These are also relevant when we consider questioning in the remote classroom.

Seven Habits of Highly Effective Questioners

Asking fewer questions
Using wait time
Differentiating questions
Selecting students
Questioning for depth
Giving useful feedback
Questioning for breadth

As you consider these habits, you'll see that, just as they are applicable in a physical classroom, they are applicable in remote learning. Your questions will be more successful if you plan them in advance and allow for a variety of types. There are several ways to think about questions.

FIRE Questions

First, Yilin Sun (2020) shares that teachers can create FIRE questions.

FIRE Questions

Factual Thinking Questions

Insightful Thinking Questions, which asks students to look at the big picture or assumptions, interpret information or give different perspectives, focus on depth and look for solutions to situations or problems.

Rational Questions, which ask students to analyze connections among both facts and implicit assumptions or focus on breadth.

Evaluative Questions, in which students focus on feelings and values that affect decisions, interpretations or analyses.

Three Classifications

In their book *Asking Better Questions* (2006), Norah Morgan and Juliana Saxton classify questions by function. They propose three types of questions: Questions That Elicit Understanding, which draw out known information; Questions That Shape Understanding, which ask for thoughts and feelings; and Questions That Press for Reflection, which require critical and creative thought. Within each classification, there are specific types of questions.

Classification	Types of Questions (Questions That . . .)
Questions That Elicit Information	• Establish the rules of the game • Establish procedure • Establish or help control group discipline • Unify the class • Focus on recall of facts • Supply information and may suggest implications
Questions That Shape Understanding	• Reveal experience • Focus on making connections • Press students to rethink or restate by being more accurate and specific • Help promote expression of attitudes, biases and points of view • Demand inference and interpretation • Focus on meanings beyond textual content
Questions That Press for Reflection	• Develop suppositions of hypotheses • Focus on personal feelings • Focus on future action or projection • Develop critical assessment or value judgments

Teaching Students to Ask Questions

It's also important to teach students how to ask questions and reflect on their thinking. Heather Clayton, in *The Art of Questioning: The Student's Role*, provides ten keys to teaching students to ask meaningful questions.

Keys to Teaching Students to Ask Meaningful Questions

Establish an environment where it is safe to ask questions.
Promote student ownership of discussions.
Model process by thinking-alouds.
Provide stems to get started.
Encourage use of open-ended questions.

Co-construct charts of student-generated questions.

Teach students where to find answers to their questions.

Provide time and means for students to seek answers.

Teach ways to help students organize their questions and thinking on paper.

Expect students to have more questions as they acquire new learning.

Question Stems or Starters

Heather points out the importance of providing stems to jump-start student questioning. When I was a teacher, I used the process of cubing, in which students roll a die or cube and use the prompt on the side to create a question. It may have been as simple as who, what, when, where, why and how, or it may have been more complex. You can tailor the questions to your needs.

Sample Question Starters

What might happen if . . .

Who did . . .

When would . . .

Why do you think . . .

How would it be different if . . .

Do you agree . . .

What evidence . . .

How does this apply . . .

In a remote setting, you can adapt cubing. First, prepare a list of starters numbered from 1 to 6. As students are working together in a small group, students can roll the virtual die using a website such as random.org. They check their number against the list and use the question starter to ask a question to their group.

Asking and Answering a Question

Finally, there were times that my students would answer a question but were unable to tell me why they knew the answer.

I was frustrated, because I wanted them to not only explain their answer but provide supportive evidence. I found that using a graphic organizer to help them chart their process was helpful, which can be completed through a shared document.

My Question	Information From My Peers	Information From My Teacher	Information I Found (list source)	Answer(s) to My Question

A Final Note

Successful planning allows you to ensure students are working at rigorous levels, but that your lessons are designed to effectively meet the needs of your students in a remote learning setting. Lesson models, general considerations for planning and incorporation of effective questioning will help you create positive learning experiences for your students.

Points to Ponder

Use the following sentence starters to reflect on the chapter.

- ◆ I learned . . .
- ◆ I'd like to try . . .
- ◆ I can adapt this strategy to my own remote teaching by . . .
- ◆ I need . . .
- ◆ I'd like to share something from this chapter with . . .

3

Expectations in the Remote Classroom

Expectations are foundational to a rigorous classroom, and include the expectations you have for your students, the expectations students have for themselves and the expectations students have for each other.

> ### *Expectations*
> Teacher to Student
> Student to Self
> Student to Student

In this chapter, we'll look at the characteristics of a culture of high expectations, teacher behaviors that reflect high expectations, reinforcing effort and assignments that reflect high expectations.

Characteristics of a Culture of High Expectations

When I was teaching at the university level, I worked with the Southern Regional Education Board. Although their strategies that create a culture of high expectations are older (2004), I find their work to be important, and while still timely, the challenge is to incorporate their recommendations into remote learning.

Strategies That Create a Culture of High Expectations

1. Classroom Management and Motivation Plans
2. Bell-to-Bell Teaching
3. Classroom Organization
4. High Expectations
5. Communicating High Expectations
6. Actively Engaging Students
7. Keeping Students on Target
8. Providing Relevant Feedback
9. Grading Practices
10. Managing Behavior Issues

Implementing these ten strategies ensures that the focus builds deeper learning experiences.

Strategies That Create a Culture of High Expectations	Applications to Remote Learning
1. Classroom Management and Motivation Plans	1. Incorporate student motivation (value and success) in lessons; create and utilize clear routines.
2. Bell-to-Bell Teaching	2. Maximize learning time with a focus on outcomes rather than the clock.
3. Classroom Organization	3. Create and utilize clear routines; organize learning tasks and resources.
4. High Expectations	4. Create opportunities for students to participate in high-level assignments, tasks and assessments.
5. Communicating High Expectations	5. Use language that shares your rigorous expectations through all materials, videos and feedback.
6. Actively Engaging Students	6. Incorporate the aspects of remote learning that can enhance engagement, such as chats.

Strategies That Create a Culture of High Expectations	Applications to Remote Learning
7. Keeping Students on Target	7. Build routines that help students stay on track, self-monitor and provide information so you can assess progress.
8. Providing Relevant Feedback	8. With remote learning, feedback is even more important. Be sure it is laser-focused on your objectives and provides information students can immediately use.
9. Grading Practices	9. Consider traditional grading but adapt it to match remote learning practices.
10. Managing Behavior Issues	10. Create protocols for behavior management, such as anti-bullying guidelines.

Teacher Behaviors That Reflect High Expectations

Teachers' beliefs, reflected in actions, demonstrate their expectations for their students. In other words, teachers treat students differently dependent on "expectancy," or what they expect. Although the difference in treatment may not be intentional, students notice it and will meet those expectations no matter how high or low they are (Williamson, 2012).

How do our behaviors reflect our expectations? For example, teachers tend to probe students more if they have high expectations. This sends a clear message that "I know you know the answer, and if I give you hints, you will formulate a reasonable response." Teachers also demonstrate expectations in the types of assignments or activities implemented in the classroom. Melissa remembers a time when her gifted students participated in thought-provoking activities such as Socratic seminars, whereas her "general classes" were given texts with questions to answer and had very little opportunity to share their various perspectives. As described by Robert Marzano (2010), let's look at typical behaviors related to low and high expectations of students.

Differential Treatment of High- and Low-Expectancy Students		
	Affective Tone	*Academic Content Interactions*
Negative	Less eye contact Smile less Less physical contact More distance from student's seat Engage in less playful or light dialogue Use of comfort talk (that's okay, you can be good at other things) Display angry disposition	Call on less often Provide less wait time Ask less challenging questions Ask less specific questions Delve into answers less deeply Reward them for less rigorous responses Provide answers for students Use simpler modes of presentation and evaluation Do not insist that homework be turned in on time Use comments such as "Wow, I'm surprised you answered correctly" Use less praise
Positive	More eye contact Smile more More physical contact Less distance from student's seat Engage in more playful or light dialogue Little use of comfort talk (that's okay, you can be good at other things)	Call on more often Provide more wait time Ask more challenging questions Ask more specific questions Delve into answers more deeply Reward them for more rigorous responses Use more complex modes of presentation and evaluation Insist that homework be turned in on time Use more praise

Let's focus on the affective aspects of high expectations as they relate to remote learning. Marzano identifies increased eye contact and smiling, more physical contact, less distance from a student's seat, playful or light dialogue and little use of comfort talk. In a remote learning setting, some of these are still applicable, especially when we present in a video setting. For eye contact, it's important to look directly in the camera. When I presented at my first Skype session, a teacher emailed me and said, "You looked down the whole time!" I was surprised, but then realized what happened. I was looking at the group on the screen, which appeared to the teachers as me looking down. It's also important that we smile, even if we are stressed. Part of our job in remote learning is to build a connection with students, which we will discuss in Chapter 7. Although you can't change your physical contact or distance, you can adjust your "virtual distance." If we sit too far away from the camera, it creates the perception of distance from the student, so we need to be closer to the screen. Although light dialogue is important, I would caution you that humor does not always translate as well on the screen, so be sure it is accompanied by a smile. Finally, when it comes to comfort talk, this can sometimes simply come across as low-expectation statements. Take a look at the following samples.

High-Expectation Statements	Low-Expectation Statements
She can definitely do better, especially with my help. He didn't understand today, but I know he can get it! She tried her best, and if she continues to work hard, she'll get better. Even though he doesn't have support at home, he continues to do his best. I know she didn't do her best. I need to work with her so she'll know what to do next time.	He can't help it. She's done the best she can do. It really is okay. I know he's trying, but he just doesn't get it. Now that I've met her parents, I know why she's the way she is. It's really not his fault he didn't do well on the project. Maybe math just isn't her subject.

Next, let's turn our attention to academic content interactions. Marzano describes high-expectation behaviors that include teachers who call on students more often, provide more wait time, ask more challenging questions and more specific questions, delve into answers more deeply, reward them for more rigorous responses and use more praise, use more complex modes of presentation and evaluation and insist that homework be turned in on time. Calling on students and providing wait time are most applicable to live presentations. The use of polls and chats allow for ample opportunities for all students to respond. When I use polls, I ask, then repeat the question, then count to 20 in my head to give everyone time to respond.

At times, I will share some related information while teachers respond, but that may be distracting for your students. Your goal is to allow all students to participate rather than rewarding the fastest typist.

Questioning aspects, including challenge, specificity and follow-up, are issues that are more related to planning, which we discussed in Chapter 2. It's important to create rigorous tasks and activities, and we'll look at that later in this chapter. Providing follow-up questions can happen via video just as it does in a school-based classroom, but you'll also want to consider how to respond in live presentation chats or small-group chat rooms. Rewarding students for more rigorous responses and using more praise is a skill you likely have, and you'll simply want to incorporate it in video presentations and in all other aspects of communication, whether it is through an email, wiki, blog or other tool.

Using more complex modes of presentation and evaluation is inherent in remote learning. You have either chosen (or been thrown into) remote learning. Finding ways to capitalize on the art of teaching, whether you are using Google Docs, Zoom, SeeSaw, wikis or any other tools, provides you the opportunity to teach with complexity. Finally, Marzano notes the importance of homework. Frankly, after talking to many teachers, my perspective is that traditional homework simply isn't a priority. Remote learning provides a variety of learning opportunities for students to complete on their own, and some type of additional "homework" is something I would not use.

Reinforcing Effort

Encouraging and reinforcing effort are particularly critical for those students who do not understand the importance of their own efforts. In *Classroom Instruction that Works*, Marzano, Pickering and Pollock (2001) make two important comments regarding students' views about effort.

Research-Based Generalizations About Effort

◆ Not all students realize the importance of believing in effort.

◆ Students can learn to change their beliefs to an emphasis on effort.

(Marzano et al., 2001, p. 50)

This is positive news for teachers. First, we're not imagining it—students don't realize they need to exert effort. And second, we can help them change that belief. Once again, this is particularly important in the remote classroom, especially when students are expected to be self-directed. Richard Curwin describes seven specific ways to encourage effort, and I've provided ideas for use in the remote classroom.

Seven Ways to Encourage Effort	*Application to the Remote Classroom*
1. Never fail a student who tries, and never give the highest grades to one who doesn't.	1. Incorporate a student's effort into your feedback on an ongoing basis, and remind students that effort is important.
2. Start with the positive.	2. Throughout the materials you provide and any video presentations, be positive about the role of effort; give students specific examples of their efforts.
3. See mistakes as learning opportunities, not failures.	3. Whenever possible, redirect students to moving past an error or mistake. You might use an online chat or bulletin board for students to discuss a learning mistake and how they overcame it.
4. Give do-overs.	4. Build multiple opportunities to demonstrate learning into your lessons, and use appropriate technology to enhance this.
5. Give students the test before you start a unit.	5. If you are using a traditional assessment, use an electronic graphic organizer, such as a mind map, to outline what they need to do.
6. Limit your corrections.	6. Keep in mind that many students are overwhelmed by remote learning and may be frustrated. Focus on a few key aspects of learning.
7. Do not compare students.	7. We are all aware of this, but with remote learning, we need to be aware that we may subconsciously compare students based on their access to resources and support.

Assignments That Reflect High Expectations

The assignments, tasks or projects we ask students to complete reflect our expectations. I visited one classroom where the teacher was quite proud of her lesson. She said she was finally able to get her students to "create," which is listed as a high-level verb in Bloom's Taxonomy. Unfortunately, her students were creating get-well cards for a sick classmate.

Having a remote learning environment is not an excuse to make things easier and default back to basic comprehension and memorization. Rigorous learning can just as easily occur virtually, but you have to be intentional and very concise in instructions to students, perhaps allowing them more freedom to make choices on assessment products.

I find that looking at descriptors of different levels, such as Webb's Depth of Knowledge or the Cognitive Rigor Matrix, are more helpful. Let's look at a variety of lessons for elementary, middle and high schools. You'll see the assignment, as well as descriptors for the level of rigor.

Example One: Close Reading Research and Writing With K–1

After reading our book about ants, let's read "The Queen Ant's Birthday" and look for evidence of the different types of ant characters. Who are the worker bees and guard bees, and what do they do for Queen Ant? How does the queen function like the queen bee in our nonfiction book? How do these bees live in community? What can we learn about living in community with one another from these two texts? In addition to using evidence from the texts, provide real-life examples to support your responses.

*Idea adapted from ReadingA-Z.com

In this example, two accessible texts are being paired, requiring a more complex level of analysis and evaluation. Not only do students need to acquire information in the first piece, they must also establish connections between the two different genres and make extended connections to how the same societal roles play out in our communities. This type of assignment could easily apply to any social studies reading as well.

Example Two: Exploring a Theme in Grades 4–5

After reading a series of short stories or poems on friendship, determine common themes that seem to recur. Create a parallel chart or semantic feature analysis of four of the texts, noting commonalities and differences in plot, characters, conflict, etc. Write a brief analysis of each story/poem, concluding with an overarching theme that connects them. Justify your ideas with textual evidence from the texts.

Finally, decide how this theme is present in your own life. As the protagonist in your own story, to what degree are you learning this life lesson?

In this example, students are asked to make connections across several literary texts and identify a theme that appears in each of the stories (nonfiction, fiction and poetry). They must develop a rationale for their chosen theme by using textual evidence from each story. Finally, they go beyond the text by applying this theme to their own life and determining whether they are learning from the wisdom in the theme. This could also be easily adapted to social studies with any topic that involves themes.

Example Three: Research and Writing in English/Language Arts or Social Studies

Choose a controversial issue of interest to you (or from an assigned time period/political platform). Use credible sources to research the various perspectives surrounding the topic. Based on the information learned, explain two or more possible solutions to the controversy that would address the key aspects of the issue. Finally, write a logical argument that contains a proposal/compromise to satisfy groups on both sides of the conflict. In your argument, be sure to explain how you will address the problem and justify your solution with logic and evidence from research.

There are several characteristics of a rigorous assignment reflected in this example. First, students are required to evaluate the credibility of sources, which is an aspect of reasoning as they consider the validity and relevance of each source. Next, they must synthesize information from numerous sources and explain possible solutions before developing a compromise that would appease all opposing viewpoints. Finally, they must use evidence from their research to justify their solution and explain how they will accomplish it.

Example Four: Exploring Perspectives/Dinner Parties

Imagine a dinner party with esteemed guests such as Stalin, Truman, Churchill and Eleanor Roosevelt. Using your knowledge of the Yalta, Potsdam and Tehran conferences in the 1940s, write a script in which these historical figures converse about their different views of what the world would look like after World War II. Choose a character and role-play this scenario, keeping the original integrity of your guest intact. At your dinner party, be sure to include what each historical figure would say about the state of society today.

In this example, students must take information they have learned and go beyond the knowledge gained to internalize the information and use it in another format. Students are stepping into a role-play scenario, using evidence and reasoning to generate a hypothetical conversation between people with opposing viewpoints while maintaining the essence of the person's true personality. Finally, they are taking the knowledge about each of the persons and applying it to a current situation, which also requires them to move beyond the text, which in this case, is what they have learned. While this assignment uses historical figures, it could easily be used with characters from a novel.

Example Five: English/Language Arts—Create a Utopia

We have been reading dystopian novels. You have been given the opportunity to start a new society on a deserted island that is fully equipped with all needed amenities and modern technology. The island is not owned or under the influence of any nation. It is the responsibility of your group to inhabit the island in any manner that you choose. By completing the following assignments and working cooperatively, your group will build the perfect society and will introduce your society to the class.

- ◆ Note the characteristics of healthy societies and governments (past and present) through online research.
- ◆ Note the pitfalls of unhealthy societies and governments (past and present) through online research.
- ◆ Determine the criteria you think would make the perfect society (type of government, freedoms, laws, technology available, etc.).
- ◆ Create a multimedia campaign advertising your community to the rest of the world. Use persuasive appeals, but justify your choices with evidence from research you conducted and the books we have read in book clubs.

In this particular example, students have just completed reading various dystopian novels in a book club format. In mixed groups, they will share what worked or didn't work in the book they read before researching societies and governments from the past and present together. The goal here is to discern the qualities that allow a society to thrive versus those that seem to indicate flaws in infrastructure of the government. Afterwards, they will self-select qualities and norms from the various governments researched to establish the criteria for a perfect society from their perspective. Students will use research-based evidence to produce a campaign using various forms of media (i.e., short video, blog, visual advertisement, interview, audio, etc.) that will attract people to their community.

Example Six: Volume (Elementary School)

You must figure out how much cereal will fit into a cereal box without measuring the box. Three responses have been provided, and you must decide which makes more sense. Illustrate or write how you figured out which response made more sense. Justify or support your reasoning as to why the others did not make sense.

Several characteristics of a rigorous assignment are reflected here. First, students are required to recognize and explain misconceptions, which is an aspect of reasoning as they consider the appropriateness of the solutions to the problems. Next, they must verify the reasonableness of their answers and provide a sound argument in support of their response that elaborates on the real-life situations.

Example Seven: Upper Elementary Science or Social Studies

Using their knowledge of past catastrophic events that have affected the Earth and life on Earth, such as earthquakes, volcanic eruptions, weather devastations and asteroid contact, students must predict the next catastrophic event that is likely to occur. They must base their prediction on research from a minimum of three sources other than the classroom text. Additionally, they must justify their prediction using their research and real-life examples and provide information as to how, if at all, people could prevent or lessen the effects of the catastrophe.

In this example, based on the range of events that happen across the world, students must make and justify a conjecture using a logical argument. Because they must research and synthesize information about past events, they are also attempting to generalize a pattern.

Example Eight: Pythagorean Theorem . . . What Is That?

Thanks to Pythagoras, we have a great equation that we can use to find the length of the sides of a right triangle. The theorem is used in architecture, navigation and surveying, which are important parts of our lives, but what if Pythagoras had never come up with the theorem? Sure, you could use measurement of a tool, but some things may be impossible to measure, such as if you are trying to find distances between long navigation points. For instance, a plane can use its height above the ground and its distance from the destination airport to find the correct place to begin a descent to that airport. But it seems like something is left out. Your charge is to come up with a replacement equation that would assist you with the following problem. You should be able to explain how you came up with the new equation and include the drawbacks of using this equation. Pythagoras can't be replaced, but I bet you can come close.

Your grandmother is moving in with you and needs wheelchair access to your home. The height of your current porch steps is 4.5 ft. Your dad said that he thinks the ramp needs to be 10 ft long. Based on your dad's guess, would you be able to build the ramp to meet these specifications? Explain how you came up with a new equation instead of the Pythagorean theorem to solve this equation. Include the drawbacks of using this equation.

https://sciencing.com/real-life-uses-pythagorean-theorem-8247514.html

In example eight, students are given a situation and are expected to develop a new solution, one that is an alternative to the Pythagorean theorem. Depending on the complexity of the situation, you might adapt this so that students are formulating a mathematical model.

Example Nine: High School Science

We have been discussing thermodynamics. Choose one of the three systems: open, closed or isolated. In your group, identify a research question based on our discussion, but one that we have not fully explored. Next, design and conduct an investigation to answer the question. Write a report in which you analyze your data, draw conclusions and cite your evidence.

You'll note that in this question, students once again identify a research question, but in this case, they also are asked to design and conduct the investigation. Additionally, they must analyze the data they collected, then draw appropriate conclusions, citing supporting evidence.

Each of these can be completed electronically, using a mix of synchrounous and asynchrounous instruction. Use the variety of tools availbe to allow students to debate online, share their thoughts on a shared document, or post their information on Canvas for comments from other students.

A Final Note

A key part of rigor is high expectations. Creating a culture of high expectations, which incorporates your behaviors, your reinforcement of students' efforts and the provision of high-quality tasks will ensure your students will succeed.

Points to Ponder

Use the following sentence starters to reflect on the chapter.

- ◆ I learned . . .
- ◆ I'd like to try . . .
- ◆ I can adapt this strategy to my own remote teaching by . . .
- ◆ I need . . .
- ◆ I'd like to share something from this chapter with . . .

4

Scaffolding and Support in the Remote Classroom

In a traditional classroom, we are able to closely monitor our students to see if they need extra help. Although that is challenging, it is even more so in a remote learning situation. Adapting effective scaffolding strategies to a remote setting will allow students to learn at higher levels. We'll look at six strategies.

Six Support and Scaffolding Strategies

Gradual Release
Graphic Organizers
Guide-o-Ramas
Optimize Strategic Learning
Technology for Specific Support
Emphasize Good Reading Habits

Gradual Release

It's important to realize that support should be used at an appropriate level through the learning process. At the beginning of new learning, more support is needed. However, as the learning continues, we want students to become more independent in their learning. This is called gradual release, and it is especially important with remote learning. Since you are not physically available at all times, we'll need to readjust our thinking with gradual release.

One way to think about scaffolding is with a diamond, or rhombus. As you can see from the following figure, it starts with me (meaning the teacher). You begin by modeling a lesson. This might happen during a live lesson, or you might record something students may refer to regularly. Next, we go to us. There are two parts of this. First is the teacher and the students (us) following guided practice. In a remote learning setting, the most effective option for this step is to work together in a synchronous setting, which allows for immediate feedback.

The second part of guided practice is "us," meaning students working with partners or in small groups. Here, you'll ideally use chats so students can work together at the same time, or as a second option, you might use some type of bulletin board setting, such as Reddit. However, since students are working back and forth on their own timelines, this is not as effective. Finally, the student (you) does the work independently, which can happen in a variety of remote formats.

How do you decide when to move a student through the various stages of gradual release? I wish I could give you a set formula, but there isn't one. Sometimes students need to see you model something once; other students may need multiple explanations and models. Capitalizing on technology can be helpful. For example, you might record your live presentation and also provide another video or set of directions to help them understand the learning practice. While observing their group or paired work, use formative assessment strategies to help you know when they are ready to work on their own. For example, when teaching students how to complete research, it's important to use a platform that allows you to share your screen and record you looking for credible,

Me, Us, You Diamond

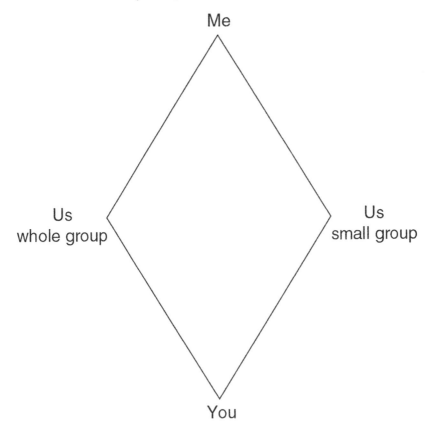

relevant sites using various key word searches and thinking aloud. Another example might be how to take the research gathered, organize it and paraphrase the information (or directly quote it), all while talking through the process with students as you make decisions to build your paragraph from research. It doesn't have to be anything fancy; students need to see that rough drafts are messy and that they take much time and thought.

When I am modeling strategies such as research skills, I find it helpful to record the session. This allows students to refer back to the content as needed.

Graphic Organizers

Graphic organizers are simply a visual way for students to organize their learning. They are particularly effective when students are working independently and need a way to chunk information, whether that is in a physical or remote classroom. One of the things I like about graphic organizers is that you can find a wide variety to meet a range of needs, and you can adapt them for your own needs. Let's look at samples from the four core content areas.

MATH

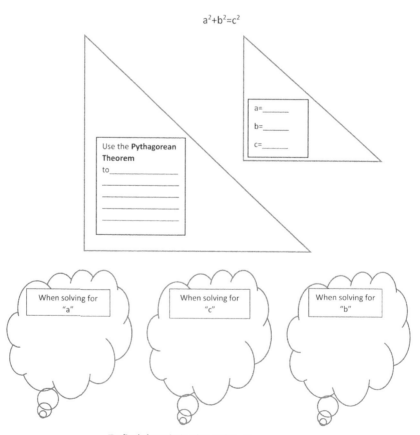

READING

Grades K–2 Semantic Feature Analysis Chart for Fables			
	Are the Characters Animals?	*Lesson Learned? (Moral)*	*Trickster?*
The Tortoise and the Hare			
The Little Boy Who Cried Wolf			
The Lion and the Mouse			

SCIENCE

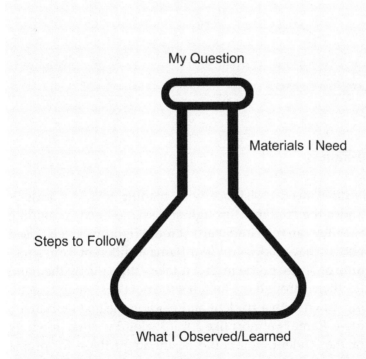

My Question

Materials I Need

Steps to Follow

What I Observed/Learned

SOCIAL STUDIES

PERSIA Graphic Organizer
(Political, Economic, Religious, Social, Intellectual and Area [geographic])

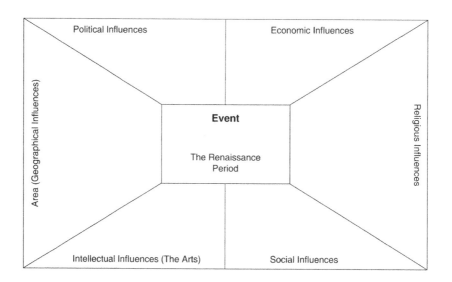

Guide-o-Ramas

Students often need assistance with reading text. A Guide-o-Rama guides the students through an assigned text, providing support so they can read and learn at more rigorous levels. Used by students as they read, a Guide-o-Rama is different from a regular outline or study guide in that it takes students by the hand and walks them through the text. It's the next best thing to actually sitting down with a student and reading the text with them. The Guide-o-Rama is almost like a think-aloud written down on paper for the student. You could easily adapt these for online learning. Using Educreation, Flipgrid, whiteboard.fi, EdPuzzle or even Google Slides, you can record on screen a section of text and then pose the question or task you would like for the students to consider before moving on to the next section of text.

How to Build a Guide-o-Rama

1. Identify a chunk of content you need students to read. Guide-o-Ramas should be used with challenging texts that you anticipate students will struggle with.
2. Determine guiding questions that will help them process key portions of the text, similar to what you would use in a traditional study guide.
3. Add "think-aloud" comments, such as, "Notice that on page 56, there is a key that explains what the map symbols represent. When I see a box of text in the margin of the text, I pay special attention, since it usually contains important information." These are typically statements and/or questions that you would verbally use to model your thinking for students.
4. Use visuals that will help students remember the content. For example, if students are learning about the characteristics of two countries, give them a graphic organizer that has outlines of the two countries rather than a simple chart.
5. Keep in mind that your goal is twofold: help students process and understand the complex text and move toward independence in learning.

The following is an example of a Guide-o-Rama that could be used with a fourth- or fifth-grade-level social studies textbook.

Guide-o-Rama **Women in the Civil Rights Movement (www.loc.gov/collections/ civil-rights-history-project/articles-and-essays/women-in-the- civil-rights-movement/)** ***This article can also be heard through an audio link.***	
Paragraph #	*Reading Tip*
1.	Paragraph 1 provides an overview and background knowledge about this topic, so I write a note to myself as to what the article is about and why it is important. Also, I think about if any of this information is true today.

| 2. | As I started reading this, I wondered what the *Student Nonviolent Coordinating Committee* and *Mississippi Freedom Summer Project* were, so I searched for them. What did you find out about each? Next, what does Gwendolyn Zoharah Simmons say about gender equality? |
| 5. | Mildred Bond Roxborough talks about the role of women in the NAACP. Do you agree with her statement "without the women, we wouldn't have an NAACP"? Search for more information and describe what you learned. |

Guide-o-Ramas are also effective for videos. With remote learning, students are viewing videos on their own, and they may not know how to watch the video or what to look for.

Guide-o-Rama **Ratios (https://youtu.be/UxWsY59NVgc)**	
Time #	*Reading Tip*
0 seconds	What do you already know about ratios? Before I watch a video, I also write down what I'm confused about or what I want to learn.
15 seconds	How does the tutor define ratios? How does it compare to your thoughts? For me, sometimes it doesn't match, so I know I need to pay extra attention to the video.
51 seconds	The first time I watched this, I was a little confused because writing a ratio looks exactly like writing a fraction. Did this confuse you?
1:40	Stop and think for a minute. Is this making sense? If it is confusing, you might want to back up the video now and rewatch it. I've found that it helps me to stop when I don't understand a step rather than waiting until the end.

I've found that written Guide-o-Ramas are effective beginning at second grade. If you think the Guide-o-Rama is too complex for your students, number or lessen the steps.

Optimize Strategic Learning

Many of our students can't focus on the content when they don't understand the strategy they should use for learning. We need to help them optimize their strategic knowledge in order to be motivated to learn. This is particularly true with remote learning, since they may not be familiar with essential strategies.

One strategy that many students struggle with is determining what's important to remember. They will highlight everything or try to write down what you say word for word. They will also only remember the trivial facts from a piece of text. It takes a lot of practice for them to start understanding "what's important" in a lesson, video, text, or activity. You might have them write headlines sometimes. They have to capture the mood and emotion of the text or subject matter and the most important event, advice or information in a news-style headline. This is a formative assessment technique that allows the teacher to see who is able to key in on the most important "ingredients" of the day.

You also might use PowerPoint or Prezi to put information up on a screen. However, some students simply copy the PowerPoint rather than identifying specific information. I recommend teaching students several strategies using a platform such as Zoom.

Steps for Identifying Specific Information

1. Discuss the importance of identifying the most important information.
2. Show students a section of text.
3. Model identifying three to five key words or phrases to write down.
4. Demonstrate how to write additional notes or an explanation without looking at the text.
5. Ask students to do the next sample on their own.

6. Provide additional modeling and guided practice as needed.
7. Ask students to practice during a lesson.
8. Provide feedback as to the quality of the notes.
9. Remind students as needed of the appropriate way to take notes.

What are the other essential strategies your students will need to use during remote learning? I spoke with one teacher who said it was critical that students know how to be an active learner. There are several specific steps students can take to prepare themselves for learning.

How to Be an Active Learner

1. When watching your teacher live, ask questions, either during the session or afterward (be sure to write them down so you remember).
2. If you are watching a recorded video, use one of the graphic organizers provided by your teacher to help you remember what you see.
3. Participate in all learning activities. You can learn much from your peers, which can enhance your individual learning.
4. Participation means more than listening. Ask questions, take notes and ask for help when needed.
5. Think about how everything you learn connects to something else you have learned or something in your life.

You may be thinking this isn't practical for you; it sounds like a tremendous amount of work to teach something your students should be able to do before they come to your class. I know

I thought my students should be able to take notes when I was teaching upper elementary students.

Our choice is to complain or help our students learn. The time investment pays off with an overall increased quality of responses. Ideally, you should do this at the beginning of the school year; but if you are in the middle of the school year, don't put off trying this strategy for another year. Better late than never. It really is simple: Define what you are looking for, explain it to your students and show them examples. Too often, we are so busy covering the content, we forget to do the basics of the strategic process.

When appropriate, give students the opportunity to come up with a plan on how to attack a lengthy project. Rather than automatically chunking it into smaller sections for them, ask students to give it a shot and present what they think a step-by-step plan might look like to be successful. You can offer feedback, but it empowers them to take the first step.

Technology for Specific Support

Technology can help students who are struggling to learn at higher levels. For example, English learners are often given simplified activities due to the language barrier. However, their lack of knowledge in speaking or writing English does not mean their growth in math, science or other subjects should be stifled. Technology offers a wide array of constantly evolving tools to support students who learn differently. Discovery Education online allows students the opportunity to read, watch and learn in their native language while they are learning English. Google Translate can take any text and convert it to one of 300 languages so that students can still access the content and learn at a high level.

For students with a learning disability, they can use Screen-casting, Nearpod or Flipgrid in a writing lesson. Each allows students to record themselves on any device, explaining their answer to a prompt or understanding of a text. Remember, the answers don't always have to come in the form of writing! Students who struggle with reading could use Microsoft Learning tools as a platform to break texts apart or have them read aloud to build fluency, confidence and comprehension, or Newsela and Freckle offer reading platforms that provide options for teachers to assign the same text with the same content but at various Lexile levels. Finally, Google extensions such as read and write for Google or readability, voice typing tools and the text-to-speech Chrome extension can assist you as you are creating ways to meet students' Individual Education Plans.

All of these tools will allow your special population to still have access to rigorous thinking and problem-solving.

You can also use wikis or other collaborative writing and social networking tools in your classroom. Elizabeth Edmondson, in her article "Wiki Literature Circles: Creating Digital Learning Communities" (2012), provides six options for using wikis as a part of the learning process. With some structured resources, wikis can also help students be successful.

Six Ways to Use Wikis in the Classroom

- ◆ Develop research projects and document ongoing student progress.
- ◆ Build a collaborative class annotated bibliography on assigned readings.
- ◆ Provide students with access to all instructor handouts.
- ◆ Map concepts, brainstorm and link relevant online resources.
- ◆ Facilitate presentations, instead of PowerPoint or other traditional methods.
- ◆ Collaborate on group projects and documents rather than emailing the documents back and forth between group members.

Emphasize Good Reading Habits

Finally, many of the leading researchers of reading instruction agree that strong readers apply certain core habits when making meaning of text. These habits are critical as students participate in remote learning. For example, if you provide written text for students, these habits ensure a more rigorous level of learning. When reading online, students tend to read for breadth rather than depth, and they are easily distracted by links and ads. Whatever you are using, it's important for students to use core reading habits. Though the wording may vary between experts, they are essentially the same: questioning the text, determining what's important, making inferences and predictions, visualizing, monitoring for meaning, activating prior knowledge and synthesizing information. It is important, whether teaching kindergarten or eleventh grade, or anything in between, to model these habits routinely so that students begin to use them naturally with texts they read or listen to.

Seven Habits of Strong Readers	
Questioning the Text	Teach students to constantly question what they're reading. When actively engaging with text, students should be naturally wondering "why are the boys on Mars?," "who could be the man behind the door?," "what does eager mean?," "will the horse ever be free?" and other such questions. This inquisitive nature will build interest and suspense as students encounter new texts for the first time.
Determining Importance	Teachers model, through think-alouds and discussions, how to determine the most important events and details in a text. It is oftentimes difficult for students of all ages to filter through extraneous details to really zoom in on the main idea and author's purpose for a written text.
Making Inferences/ Predictions	Students must be trained to pick up on implicit information in the text to create deeper meaning.

Seven Habits of Strong Readers, continued	
Visualizing	Good readers make a movie in their heads while reading. Provide opportunities for students to sketch out, paint and use descriptive words to create the setting and events in the texts you read with them. This may not come naturally to all learners, so teacher modeling will be important.
Monitor for Meaning	Teach students to pause while reading a text to think about and process what they have just read or heard you read. Allow them to clarify or retell what they've just heard to ensure that they're comprehending during pause points. The goal is for students to learn to do this independently.
Activate Prior Knowledge	Students will more readily grasp a concept if they have something to connect it to. Creating a schema by building background knowledge allows a reader to understand the text more deeply, leading to increased fluency and comprehension.
Synthesize	Strong readers must connect the dots while reading. Teach them to look for information in multiple places in the text and use that textual evidence in their verbal or written responses. Even young learners can do this if it is modeled for them. Synthesizing also requires students to gather evidence throughout the text to create new meaning and understanding of characters and themes.

As you reflect on the earlier part of this chapter, you may realize that graphic organizers and Guide-o-Ramas can help students learn and practice these habits. Incorporating these tools will enhance learning for all students, especially those who are struggling.

A Final Note

Support and scaffolding are essential parts of rigorous learning. They are even more important when students are learning remotely, because they do not have your immediate physical presence to observe and know when they need help. Using a variety of support and scaffolding strategies will ensure your students are successful.

Points to Ponder

Use the following sentence starters to reflect on the chapter.

♦ I learned . . .
♦ I'd like to try . . .
♦ I can adapt this strategy to my own remote teaching by . . .
♦ I need . . .
♦ I'd like to share something from this chapter with . . .

5

Demonstrating Learning in the Remote Classroom

As I work with teachers across the world, including Australia, I continue to hear the concern "There are strategies that work quite well in my classroom. How do I keep using things that work?" There are some activities that do not translate as easily to remote learning. However, there are some that, with some adjustments, can be effective. In this chapter, we'll look at four ways to demonstrate learning in a remote classroom.

> Academic Discourse
> Document-Based Questioning
> Exploring Various Perspectives
> Virtual Experiences

Academic Discourse

Much of what we have discussed throughout the book involves student discussion. However, there is a difference between "student talk" and academic discourse. Talk typically is at a surface level and oftentimes veers off topic. Academic discourse, on the other hand, is focused on the content and incorporates academic vocabulary.

There are several common problems with classroom discussion.

Problems With Student Talk in the Classroom

◆ Controlled by teacher
◆ Too little student talk
◆ Too focused on simply answering teacher's questions
◆ Veers off topic
◆ Surface level rather than in depth
◆ Dominated by a few students, typically excluding struggling students

---

These occur whether you are in an in-class physical setting or in a remote one. It's important to build structure and scaffolding into class discussions to address these problems.

If we want to incorporate discourse into our classroom, we cannot assume that it will automatically occur. In addition to teaching students what to discuss, we need to provide and teach a set of norms explaining how to discuss. For primary students, choose three to four norms that are easy to remember and post them with pictures or symbols for visual cues. For example, for younger students, you might use *Listen to Everyone*, *Wait Your Turn* and *Mistakes Are Okay*.

Sample Classroom Norms for Discourse

◆ We are all a team, so we work together rather than competing.
◆ We respect each other and act appropriately.
◆ We actively listen to each other, which allows us to authentically contribute our perspectives.
◆ If you don't agree with someone, find a positive way to respond without embarrassing the other person.

◆ Everyone should be able to participate. If one person is talking too much, the other group members should give them a signal and move on.

◆ The process is just as important as the result. We want to think deeply about our work, elaborate, justify our points and pose additional questions to promote more thinking.

◆ Making mistakes is normal; it helps us learn.

◆ If you need help, check out the online Resource Board for questioning prompts and/or sample vocabulary.

The norms should be part of your overall classroom climate.

Finally, we need to look at norms that facilitate discourse in a remote learning classroom. Rhonda Bondie, in her article "Practical Tips for Teaching Online Small Group Discussions," provides helpful information regarding online discussions. She notes the value of virtual breakouts, where students use Note Catcher or Google Docs to organize discussions and where the teacher can facilitate the discussion using pre-assignments and a feedback survey.

Other structures that are important include posting directions and key resources in a place that is easily accessible, encouraging students to post videos or other visuals to support the discussion and incorporating surveys into the discussion.

As I talk with teachers, they have noted other important norms related to online conversation. Discussion may occur verbally during live video sessions, or they may occur in writing. When using Google Meet, Zoom or other similar applications, you'll want to establish clear guidelines for remaining muted and raising a hand to speak.

In an asynchronous setting, students need instruction on how to have a virtual conversation and exhibit the behaviors of a responsible digital citizen. For example, students will need to learn how to provide timely responses, which should both validate responses and challenge the response when appropriate.

Another issue during online discussion is teacher involvement, which is critical. You'll want to listen to the discussion and add feedback, but it's important to structure how you do so. I was very clear with my graduate students that I would listen, but that I would not post a response immediately. I learned early on that if I immediately posted a response to each comment, it limited the students' comments. They would wait to see what I would say before they replied. I would comment throughout the discussion, but after I gave students "electronic wait time." Be sure to share what you are doing with students and parents.

Finally, although there are a wide range of tools that can facilitate discussion, some are particularly helpful with classroom discussion. One option that allows for open conversation in a secure, private chatboard is kialo.com. This platform allows teachers to pose a question or idea and have students respond with evidence from outside sources to support their thoughts. They can also respond to one another's "evidence" and thoughts, creating healthy academic dialogue. Primarily marketed as a debate platform, it can be used to discuss literature, scientific hypothesis or many other content topics. YoTeach is a similar tool that allows teachers to open chat rooms as a whole class or in small groups. This allows for real-time conversation between students, with the ability for the teacher to moderate and redirect if necessary. Flipgrid allows for visible discussion as students create short videos in response to a topic the teacher publishes. Peers can then submit response videos, and students can have dialogue "face to face." Reluctant writers enjoy this option, as it allows them to speak about their thoughts and contribute without their writing skills holding them back. Each of these can enhance student learning.

Document-Based Questioning

One way for students to process learning through writing is document-based questioning (DBQ), which has become popular in recent years. Although I will focus on the use of DBQ in English/language arts and social studies classrooms, it is easily adaptable to science classrooms and can also be used with math text.

DBQ prompts students to answer a question that requires them to state a claim and support it with evidence, analysis and reasoning.

However, DBQ thinking does not have to be reserved for middle and high school students. DBQ Project researchers observed numerous classrooms, from kindergarten through fifth graders, and found that young school children are capable of evidence-based thinking and writing (www.dbqproject.com/). Based on this, the DBQ Project developed a concept referred to as Mini-Qs, which offer primary source documents, background texts and a controlling question for elementary students. More commonly used in social studies classrooms, Mini-Qs are also useful in language arts classrooms. In our language arts classrooms, we found that students would simply look for events that occurred during a piece of literature to answer a question. In a Mini-Q, students need to make an argument by moving beyond summarizing events to deeper analysis of the text.

Four Key Components

There are four key components of the DBQ and Mini-Qs: the question, supporting texts and documents, the instruction that provides students scaffolding to be successful and the assessment criteria. NowComment provides an online tool that allows teachers to post images and documents that students can discuss, with or without DBQ prompts. Students can also post content, so they are able to contribute to the discussion.

The first component of DBQ is designed to require students to make an argument, supporting it with evidence and justification. Then, students work with the corresponding document.

Sample ELA Document-Based Question	Sample Social Studies Document-Based Question
Question: How did the Civil War, increased number of immigrants and the economy of our country affect children of the late 1800s and early 1900s?	Question: Why did the colonies almost fail to thrive?
Documents/Texts: *The Boxcar Children* books Historical photos from the early 1900s of orphan trains Nonfiction picture books about orphan trains Diary entry of an orphan who experienced the orphan train	Documents/Texts: Topographical map of the original 13 colonies Original letter (read aloud by teacher) from a colonist about the conditions Historical record of climate/weather along the Eastern Coast Picture books on the colonies

Sample Document Types for ELA Classrooms	Sample Document Types for Social Studies Classrooms
Excerpts from texts Short stories Videos Simulations Poems Diary entries Photographs Artwork	Primary source documents Excerpts from texts Videos Simulations News articles (Scholastic Kids is great) Political cartoons (age-appropriate) Photographs

When I first talked with teachers about DBQs, my question was how they were providing the documents to students, since many of the documents were not found online. I found that it varies, depending on the school and district. As long as you follow copyright protocols, you may be able to scan pages to create an electronic document for students. Several schools I spoke with purchase the electronic rights, which can be cost prohibitive. Finally, there are districts that provide paper documents to students if they cannot access electronic ones.

Third, students need appropriate instruction to support the process. This may occur during whole-class video presentations or small-group coaching and during full lessons or mini-lessons. In order for students to work at rigorous levels, such as providing justification for conclusions and going beyond the text to make connections, you can provide recorded or live mini-lessons on key strategies.

Sample Mini-Lessons to Support DBQ

◆ Making observations vs. making inferences.
◆ Distinguishing between fact and opinion.
◆ Using outside knowledge to draw conclusions.
◆ Identifying primary vs. secondary source material.

Regardless of age or reading level, using documents to support and enrich learning in your classroom is beneficial; in fact, they will help students gain deeper access to texts that may be too difficult to understand in isolation. Coupled with rich classroom discussion, this level of engagement will increase the rigor in your classroom.

Finally, assessment allows you to see if students have developed a deep level of understanding. One of the most important elements in a DBQ assessment is a rubric that defines your criteria for quality work. This will provide a clear description for assessment and for formal grading.

Exploring Various Perspectives

An important life and career skill is the ability to analyze different perspectives of an issue. After students graduate, whether they begin a career, join the military or attend some type of higher education, they will be asked to problem-solve, which requires looking at a variety of options and making the best decision based on that comparison. We can help students develop that skill while working in a remote setting.

RAFT

An introductory activity for students to look at different perspectives is through RAFT (Santa, Havens, & Macumber, 1996). RAFT stands for Role, Audience, Format and Topic. Using this strategy, students would assume a role (such as an astronaut vs. a NASA technician) and write from that perspective to a more authentic audience, such as people reading his or her online blog. With a slight shift in the assignment details, students are required to understand the topic at a higher level in order to complete the task. Additionally, when students are asked to write for a genuine purpose and audience, they tend to complete the assignment more effectively. As you can see from the examples, you can tailor this task to remote learning by altering the format. For younger students, they can draw rather than write their RAFTs.

Role	Audience	Format	Topic
Right triangle	Students	Virtual tour	Why Pythagoras was important
Comma	Young authors	Op-ed piece	Misuses of the comma
Water drop	New water drops	Travel guide	Water cycle
Musical note	Composer	Persuasive letter	Usefulness in symphony
Computer programmer	Venture capitalist (funding provider)	Design for new video game	Conflict in the Middle Ages

Moving Into Debates

An activity that allows students to actively participate in debate activities is I Think/You Think.

In the upper elementary or middle grades, students, working individually or in small groups, must research a topic thoroughly enough to be able to anticipate and refute an argument in an instant. Small groups can occur in breakout chat or video rooms or through a shared document. It is important to provide structure for groups, which includes guidelines for participation and a timeline.

Former teacher Lindsay Yearta used an early form of debate to teach her students to see different perspectives on an issue. She begins with a handout that includes a statement: "I am for/against (insert your topic here)." Next, she assigns each student a position (for or against). The students circle their position on a handout and then research three reasons to support their position. She says,

They get into their groups and come up with what they think the other group would say. What do you think their points are going to be? Then, they write down at least three points their opposition might have and they research comebacks to the opposition's points. They have to think ahead and research not only their position, but the other side as well. Then, when we hold our debate, each student had to speak at least once.

The verbal exchange is supported by the depth of research on both points of view. To increase rigor, students must support and justify their claims with research, testimonials, textual evidence, etc.

In primary grades, after reading two books or stories, students can say (in a virtual or recorded session), "This book is better because . . ." Then a student who prefers a different book can respond. You can also expand this to high school by increasing the depth of your expectations.

Depending on your technology resources, students can debate in a chat setting, through a series of blog entries or text messages or using platforms such as DebateArt.

Sample Debate Topics

◆ After reading *The One and Only Ivan*, do you think zoos should be banned?
◆ Is remote learning better than being in our school building?
◆ Should companies be allowed to make a profit at the expense of the rainforest?
◆ Would we be better off if we were not required to learn algebra?

Finally, students can look at a variety of perspectives, rather than limiting themselves to two viewpoints. In this case, students explore a topic online, using recommended resources if needed for scaffolding, and create "fake" social media accounts for all perspectives. Programs and apps are available for teachers and students, or you can ask students to design their own in a Google Doc. Other students review the content, similar to a gallery walk, and add their thoughts in response.

Points of View			
Topic	*View 1*	*View 2*	*View 3*
Lunch menu	Cafeteria workers	Student who loves junk food	Student who wants to eat healthy food
Election	Political candidate 1	Political candidate 2	Voter
Solar system	Copernicus	Contemporaries of Copernicus	Sun
Musical score	Conductor	Musicians	Audience member
Art	Sculptor or painter	Piece of art	Person looking at art
Word problems in math	The missing number or variable	The solution	The student trying to solve the problem

Virtual Experiences

In today's technological world, I would be remiss to not mention the opportunity that the growing field of virtual reality (VR) offers. VR is an ideal strategy for remote classrooms. Monica Burns, founder of ClassTechTips and EdTech consultant, suggests that even if students do not have Google Cardboards or other VR devices, you can still incorporate VR into your curriculum and help students experience facets of an otherwise one-dimensional text. Instead of simply reading about the Battle of Waterloo, use an interactive whiteboard or video clip to provide the opportunity for them to see and hear a re-enactment of Napoleon's defeat by swiping all around them to see the battlefield from all angles. Allow your students the opportunity to accompany two Himalayan school girls on their daily six-hour trek to school or take a 360-degree tour of the Sphinx and pyramids at Giza. In English/language arts classes, virtually take your students to a zoo to show them the setting for *Midnight at the Zoo* or provide an opportunity for them to climb to base camp on Mt. Everest when reading the novel *Peak*. To apply math concepts, take an online tour of a city and identify the math applications to architecture or simply examples of math seen in the tour. Or, for science, students can participate in online experiments or simulations on a variety of topics. The options are endless, so take advantage of all the free material online to transform learning as your students know it.

Sources for Virtual Reality Education

National Geographic's YouTube Channel A series of 360-degree videos captures VR from any web browser and touch-screen device.

Nearpod.com Excellent VR lessons for students of all ages across all content.

Discovery Ed Hundreds of videos that transport students to locations around the world in an instant.

BBC 360° (YouTube) Allows students to experience the sights and sounds of destinations across the globe.

Google Arts and Culture Takes people inside cultural and historical events and provides street views of famous landmarks or sites (https://artsandculture.google.com /explore).

One specific way to utilize VR is through virtual field trips. However, it's important to remember that the field trip itself should not be the end result. Any tour should be linked to your standards, and the activities should result in increased learning related to your objectives. In the following sample, a visit to the Louvre was linked to a study of Egyptian history in a middle school class. With adaptations of the assignments, it could easily be used in a high school art class.

The Louvre Visit

Today we are going to take an exciting trip to Paris, France! Your ticket is www.louvre.fr/en and your vehicle is your computer, tablet or phone. Please read the instructions carefully so your trip is not wasted. I want you to have fun and learn something new in the process. We will have a round-table discussion on our magnificent trip on Friday. Have fun, and I can't wait to hear about your adventure!

1. As your tour guide, I suggest you learn some information about the Louvre Museum before you begin your tour. Start at the *Collection and Louvre Palace* link. *Read the information about the history of the Louvre. You are in Paris and you call home to talk to someone you love. Tell them about the Louvre's history in three to five sentences. Include why the museum was established and how it has been important to France.*

2. Now you are ready to take your tour. Using the same link, go to *Online Tours*. Choose the following tour: *Egyptian Antiquities. Walk around on the floor to several areas. Spend ten minutes learning how to navigate through the museum floor. Go to the help menu for ways to better navigate the tour.*

3. Choose one sculpture from your tour. Analyze how it reflects the culture of Egypt.

---

4. Interpret the artwork. Communicate the artist's statement. Describe what you think the artist is trying to say through the work of art. Expound on the feeling conveyed by the artwork. Describe what the artwork means to you and why. Explain what you feel is the artist's intended purpose for creating that particular work of art. Examine why the artist made the choices in technique, materials and subject matter and how they relate to the intended purpose. Your narrative should be approximately one page.

Note: For more suggestions, visit www.wikihow.com/Critique-Artwork (the suggestions in number 4 are an excerpt from this site).

Ideas for Other Content Areas

Math: Students can plan the trip to the Louvre, look up the flight and calculate the cost.

Social Studies: Plan what to take and how to pack, discuss how to prepare to visit the country and learn about Paris and the French government. Also discuss the history of Egypt and the symbolism of the historical time period.

Language Arts: How did the authors and poets of Egypt affect the culture? Also teach about critiques and writing the analysis.

Other examples of virtual field trips are the Smithsonian museums, aquariums, volcanoes, children's museums, famous locations such as Ellis Island or the Alamo, coral reefs or sports halls of fame. To find options that are best for your students, simply search online for "virtual field trips" and your grade range, subject or topic.

A Final Note

Finding rigorous strategies for students to demonstrate their understanding in a remote learning classroom can take time. However, you can start by taking activities that have been effective for you in the past and adjust them to your new instruction. Strategies such as academic discourse, DBQ, exploring various perspectives and virtual experiences can be adapted to remote learning.

Points to Ponder

Use the following sentence starters to reflect on the chapter.

◆ I learned . . .
◆ I'd like to try . . .
◆ I can adapt this strategy to my own remote teaching by . . .
◆ I need . . .
◆ I'd like to share something from this chapter with . . .

6

Rigorous Assessment in the Remote Classroom

Assessments are an important part of a remote classroom, and one that can be challenging. In this chapter, we'll look at both formative assessments and summative ones. Then, we will finish with a discussion of grading.

Effective Formative Assessment

Formative assessments, which are typically informal, take place throughout the instructional process. They should be administered frequently, since they provide an immediate assessment of students' levels of mastery. Andrew Miller shares seven considerations for remote learning classrooms.

Seven Considerations for Remote Learning Classrooms
Know Your Purpose
Collect Data Over Time
Focus on Feedback
Check for Understanding in Synchronous Sessions

Leverage Personal Conversations
Check In on Social Emotional Learning
Make It Useful

Source: www.edutopia.org/article/formative-assessment-distance-learning

As we discussed with the PPPR (Purpose, Product, Process, Resources) model in Chapter 2, you should always start with your purpose. In our next section on formative assessment, consider that formative data and checking for understanding should occur over time. Strategies and tools for providing feedback allow for formative assessment. Making learning useful or relevant has been embedded in the strategies throughout the book, and in the next chapter, you'll find specific information about how relevance relates to student motivation. Finally, many options for integrating conversations and social emotional learning are incorporated throughout the book.

Examples of Rigorous Formative Assessments

Let's look at a range of formative assessments that are useful in a remote learning classroom.

Checklists

An important formative assessment tool for teachers is the use of checklists. Checklists, which provide a quick way for you to make notes about your observations, can be simple yes/no tallies or they can be open-ended for teachers to add notes. You can use checklists to observe students during videos, monitor chats or other group work or review tasks or assignments.

Sample Mathematics Checklist	
Characteristic	*Notes*
Student demonstrates problem-solving ability.	

Sample Mathematics Checklist	
Characteristic	*Notes*
Student demonstrates persistence while solving problems.	
Student reflects on his/her thinking.	

Sample Language Arts Checklist	
Characteristic	*Notes*
Student demonstrates ability to write a narrative paragraph.	
Student demonstrates persistence while writing.	
Student reflects on his/her writing and makes revisions throughout the process.	
Student shows applications of simple conventions (capital letters, punctuation).	

Anticipation Guides

Anticipation guides can be used to activate prior knowledge of your students, but they also allow insight into student thinking prior to a new text or topic. I prefer to use anticipation guides with partners using a tool such as Google Docs, but you may prefer that students complete this individually.

In pre-K, students can respond by circling a smile face or frown face to let you know if they agree or disagree with the statement. You can also do it orally by asking students to hold up a card with a smile face or a frown face as you read each statement.

Anticipation Guide		
Agree/Disagree Before the Lesson	*Content*	*Agree/Disagree After the Lesson*

Connections

When teaching new content, consider pausing and asking students to create connections between the new materials and something with which they are familiar. Although very difficult for the students because of its abstract nature, it will provide insight into how closely your students are conceptualizing the new material and allow for real-life applications.

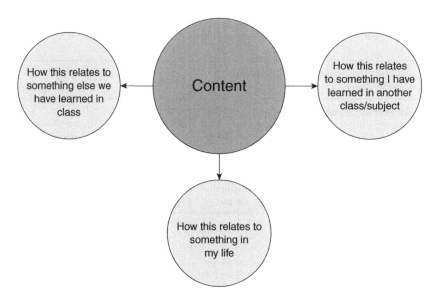

Four Corners

You can also use written chat rooms, Flipgrid or YoTeach, to provide for an academic version of Four Corners. You may ask students to go to Chat Room 1 if they strongly support the actions of Stanley Yelnats in *Holes*, Chat Room 2 if they agree, Chat Room 3 if they disagree or Chat Room 4 if they strongly disagree. They must have a rationale for their decision based on textual evidence. Similarly, you could use Four Corners to review information. After teaching about Ancient Egypt, you could assign students at random to one of four corners to collaborate with new group members: Chat Room 1—religion/gods; Chat Room 2—pharaohs and mummies; Chat Room 3—architecture/pyramids; Chat Room 4—government/social classes. These groups return to the general chat to share, at which point you can address any major points that have been missed and correct any misunderstandings. This is also an excellent option for allowing students to create multiple-choice questions for other groups.

This is also a good opportunity to mention live virtual breakout chat rooms, such as those incorporated in Zoom. While beneficial, they are difficult to monitor simultaneously. Many school or district policies require continual monitoring. Check with your school or district to see if breakout chat rooms are an option.

Sketch It Out/Describe It

Many students enjoy using pictures to demonstrate their learning. In some cases, they will actually demonstrate learning at a higher level than if they write their answers, and for primary students, it is more appropriate. In Sketch It Out, students draw their responses to a prompt. Apps such as You Doodle and Kids Doodle provide students a technology-based option for this activity.

What Matters Most

Next, the activity What Matters Most requires students to prioritize information, identifying the most important learning concepts. You can begin by listing information on a chart or shared document and having students work together to choose the most important. Over time, they can generate ranking items from most to least important.

Exit Slips

One of the most common formative assessment strategies to use after a lesson is an exit slip. However, did you know there are different types of exit slips? It's important to choose the type based on what you want to learn. Also, you may want to mix and match questions for varying types.

Types of Exit Slips

Demonstrating Understanding of Content
Reflecting on How They Processed Learning
Asking Questions
Self-Assessing Understanding

No matter what type of exit slip you are using, you'll want to find a way to manage the information. With today's technology, there is a variety of ways to collect exit slip information from your students. With any mobile device, students can access a digital platform and immediately push answers out to the teacher, who then has the ability to display the class's thinking as a whole on the screen or choose a select few to further discuss.

Electronic Exit Slips

- ◆ Google Forms
- ◆ Mentimeter
- ◆ Recap
- ◆ Plickers
- ◆ Geddit
- ◆ Poll Everywhere
- ◆ ExitTicket
- ◆ Lino
- ◆ Padlet (will soon require a fee)

Other Tools

There are many other tools that allow you to incorporate formative assessment in your classroom. Let's look at a sampling.

Formative Assessment Tools	
Online Platform	*Functions*
Padlet	• Acts as digital KWL that can be used to gather student feedback.
Socrative	• Develop quizzes, exit tickets, use before or after instruction and organizes data for teacher analysis.
Backchannelchat. com	• Pause during a lesson or reading of a text and ask everyone to comment or respond to a question or prompt.
Nearpod.com	• Push content out to student devices, one screen at a time, and allow them to interact digitally through multiple-choice questions, open-ended response, annotating text online, drawing on a blank canvas, exploring a virtual 3D image, etc. Provides a way for teachers to facilitate a lesson and get immediate real-time feedback as to what your students are thinking.

Formative Assessment Tools	
Online Platform	*Functions*
EdPuzzle	• Use any video from a myriad of online sources and insert pause points where students must gather thoughts, answer a question, make a prediction, etc., before they can continue the video. Completely customize a student-directed video lesson and gather feedback via student responses in real time.
Explaineverything. com	• Watch your students' thinking. Explain Everything is an interactive whiteboard that asks students to explain their thinking through a problem or through a prompt. Focus on quality over quantity.
Flipgrid	• Use any iOS device to create a video response to a question or prompt. Because you can't have a high-quality conversation with every student every day, this allows you to see what they know via explanation.
Kahoot	• Use gaming to review! This assessment platform is game based but allows teachers to create content and disaggregate data.
Go Formative	• Upload documents, create your own questions, embed videos or pictures and receive immediate data on student performance.

Providing Feedback to Students

Providing timely feedback to students is even more important in the remote classroom. Since you cannot verbally address a misconception as soon as you notice it, breaking large assignments down into a step-by-step, daily process will benefit students of any age. By modeling and assigning one chunk at a time, you will be able to formatively assess progress and communicate that to students before they move on to the next step. This is not a time to drop a complex assignment onto students' laps and tell them to complete it by the end of the week. While that may work for the top 10% of students, it will not work for the majority of them. Why? Because they need checkpoints to ensure that they are on the right track. When you're not physically present to provide it to them, affirming their work routinely and correcting their errors before they get too far are imperative.

The system you set up for feedback is up to you. Google Docs offers an easy way to provide feedback on student work. However, for younger ages, Flipgrid messages from teachers are well-received. It is crucial to establish office hours where students can come to ask questions and seek feedback, but for those more reluctant, I suggest inviting them to a one-on-one or small-group virtual meeting. Differentiation and flexible grouping are simple to do with remote learning, as students are not necessarily aware of what other students may or may not be doing at any given time. When you notice students making similar error patterns, take the time to provide verbal feedback through Google Meet or Zoom. Small conferences with a teacher make a powerful difference. Likewise, you could schedule one day a week for one-on-one checkpoints individually or in small, homogenous student groups. Again, being available to provide feedback routinely is critical.

That said, the teacher isn't the only one who can provide feedback. Platforms such as NowComment allow students to post documents and work and receive peer feedback. Teachers can even set up small collaboration groups in which students can have meaningful conversations centered around giving one another positive and constructive feedback. Again, this is a learned skill. We spoke about academic discourse in Chapter 5.

Summative Assessment

Now, we'll shift our attention to the critical aspects of summative assessment. You may think that summative assessments are difficult with remote learning, since students can look up the answers or ask for help. Although there are always times that can happen, a teacher I spoke with said, "I'm not worried about it. I should be providing a rigorous assignment for which students can't just look it up."

I spoke with Missy Miles, one of my former graduate students, a current teacher in Charlotte, North Carolina, and co-author of my companion books on *Rigor in the ELA and Social Studies*

Classroom (K–5 & 6–12). I wanted her perspective, both as a teacher and a parent, on this issue. Her response:

> One of the first realizations my colleagues came to when we were tossed into Distance Learning was the fact that assessment would need to look different. Many teachers take every precaution possible to prevent their students from cheating (i.e., parents signing a proctor statement, putting Chromebooks on "lock mode" virtually, requiring students to take the assessment within a given hour while on Google Meet so they could be watched, etc.). While it is important to teach the importance of academic integrity, my first thought was this, "If we have to work so hard to keep students from looking up an answer online during an assessment, then perhaps our assessments aren't moving beyond a simple memorization/ regurgitation level as they should be." Perhaps the problem lies within the types of questions we're asking and the types of skills we're asking students to demonstrate. Think about it: if a student can easily Google the answer to your questions, is your question really rigorous? The answer is most likely not. I immediately knew this would call for a much-needed revision of our assessment practices. Yes, students need to know facts; there's no way around it. But that should not be the ultimate objective. The task should not stop with a quick mention of the fact. That should only be the beginning. Assign the student a task to do with the fact. Require them to use many terms/facts/knowledge bases together to create new meaning or have them evaluate someone else's use of those facts/ terms.

In this section, we'll look at key characteristics of effective summative assessment for remote learning classrooms, as well as sample assessments that are rigorous.

Summative Assessment in Distance Learning

As I was reviewing information specific to assessment and remote learning, I once again found myself turning to Andrew Miller's work on Edutopia. He provides seven key tips to consider, but he notes these are simply strategies that can help with summative assessment, not solutions to every challenge.

Summative Assessment in Distance Learning

Stop assessing every standard. Prioritize!

Assign performance tasks.

Use a series of smaller tasks rather than one big task.

Use conversations and ask students to orally defend their opinions.

Leverage technology tools when possible.

Teach academic integrity and trust your students.

Use your professional judgment.

Source: www.edutopia.org/article/summative-assessment-distance-learning

---

As a part of developmental appropriateness, we must also address authenticity. When assessments seem contrived, they are not as effective. Let's look at this example for middle school students:

Sample Assignment

Solve a set of computational problems related to proportions, geometrical shapes and rotations.

Notice how the task is not an authentic situation for young adolescents. The rigor and authenticity would be improved if we reframed the assignment.

Revised Assignment

Choose a topic you are interested in, such as skateboarding. Create either a PowerPoint, blog or video about the relationship between your topic and math. Include at least three examples.

Test Questions

Now let's look at several types of questions that are typically used on tests and as part of your instruction.

Multiple-Choice Questions

Multiple-choice tests are probably the most common tests in classrooms across the nation. Although due in part to preparation for standardized tests, they are also easy to score. They also apply to a wide range of cognitive skills, including higher-order thinking ones. Finally, incorrect answers, if written correctly, can help you diagnose a student's problem areas. Disadvantages include that the questions can't measure a student's ability to create or synthesize information and that students can guess an answer.

Electronic Tools for Multiple-Choice Questions

Infuse Learning
Quiz Socket
Kahoot!
Quizizz
Google Forms

There are several ways to write multiple-choice questions that allow you to increase the rigor. First, choose a question that moves beyond basic recall. Next, create choices for the stem that are clearly correct or incorrect without making them too easy. In other words, if we provide examples that are clearly off topic, it makes it easier for students to guess. Although some teachers do not like to use "all of the above," "none of the above" or "a and d" options, I do find they require older students (grades four and up) to think at a higher level. Remember, you know your students; adapt our suggestions so they match your students' needs.

Let's look at a science example.

Science Example (Astronomy)

Which of the following could result in destruction of a spacecraft traveling to Mars?

a. Highly accelerated subatomic particles hit the shielded navigation system.
b. A micrometeor the size of a marble ruptures the pressurized argon fuel.
c. The spacecraft comes within 100,000 km of a black hole.
d. a and b could destroy a spacecraft.
e. a and c could destroy a spacecraft.
f. b and c could destroy a spacecraft.
g. All of the above could destroy a spacecraft.
h. None of the above could destroy a spacecraft.

Finally, let's look at an elementary math example.

Mathematics Example

For your playdate on Saturday at your house, you requested a large pizza, which consisted of 12 slices. You and your three friends ate pizza, but you also had ice cream so there are still 4 slices of pizza left. What fraction of pizza did you and your friends eat?

a. 2/3
b. 3/4
c. 8/12
d. 5/8
e. Both b and c
f. None of the above statements are accurate.

Short-Answer Questions

Short-answer questions are an expanded form of fill-in-the-blank. Responses are not as long as essays, but they usually include more than one sentence. In addition to the tools listed here, Socrative is a useful tool. You'll need to build rigor into the context of your questions. Although more challenging to grade than matching, true-false, fill-in-the-blank and multiple-choice questions, they are simpler than assessing essay questions. In the following three examples at a variety of grade levels and subjects, you'll notice that students need to move beyond a basic level of understanding. This also means that students are less likely to search for the answer on the internet.

Social Studies Example

Which of the two deserts, the Gobi or the Karakum, is easier for surviving for those who might live there and why?

English/Language Arts Example

Based on what you have read in *The Lemonade War*, compare and contrast the two siblings' personalities to someone you know in your life.

Essay Questions

Essay questions, which are sometimes considered a type of performance assessment, are one of the most common assessments used in today's classrooms. Essay questions are extremely effective for measuring complex learning. Opportunities for guessing are removed, so you can truly measure what students understand. There are several disadvantages, however, including the amount of time to grade them, the subjective nature of grading and the dependency of the answer on the student's writing ability.

When you are writing essay questions, crafting the question is particularly important. You want to be sure the complexity of the learning outcome is reflected in a clear, focused manner. It's also important to provide explicit instructions as to your expectations.

As with any question, you can write items at a lower or higher level. In our case, we want to strive for rigorous questions as much as possible. Todd Stanley, in *Performance-Based Assessment for 21st-Century Skills*, provides an excellent example of an essay question that he revised to a more rigorous version.

Standard Essay Question

What is the theme of "Goldilocks and the Three Bears"? Make sure to use details from the text to support this choice.

Rigorous Essay Question

What is the theme of "Goldilocks and the Three Bears"? Make sure to use details from the text to support this choice. "Goldilocks and the Three Bears" was written nearly 200 years ago. Justify whether this theme applies to today. Provide an example from modern life to validate your answer.

Notice that although the first question does require some higher-order thinking, the second one is at a more advanced level. It's very specific so that students know exactly what to do to demonstrate their understanding. Once again, the more rigorous example lessens the likelihood that students can copy an answer from the internet. Now, let's review three other samples.

Science Example (Interdependent Relationships in Ecosystems)

How has human behavior affected soil erosion, and how will this affect life in 20 years? What changes would you recommend, if any, to minimize the effects on erosion? Your response must be based on a minimum of three credible sources other than your textbook. Include evidence cited specifically from the sources and incorporate real-life examples and applications.

Math

Write a rule for what happens when you multiply a one-digit number by 10 that your classmates can use. Explain why your rule will always work.

Social Studies

People are sometimes forced to move from place to place to survive. Write an essay that explains the various ways nomads benefit from migrating often. Next, describe the problems they experience when moving. Finally, explain how becoming a nomad would affect you in terms of your family, friends, schools and other interests.

Performance-Based Assessments

Performances, which in many ways are more authentic, encompass a wide range of activities, some of which can be incorporated in project- and problem-based learning and portfolios. Students can post their performance-based assessments in electronic portfolios.

Tools for Electronic Portfolios

VoiceThread
Kidblog
Three Ring
EduBlog
FolioSpaces
Googlios (from Google)
Weebly
Evernote

The main distinguishing characteristic is that students perform in some manner to demonstrate understanding.

For example, Kendra Alston shared a performance activity she experienced during a high school social studies class. She wasn't excited to study the 1920s and 1930s, but her teacher, Mr. Baldwin, told them he was giving a *show me what you know* final exam. Kendra said:

> He didn't care how you showed it, as long as you showed what you know. Things flashed before my eyes, but I was into theatre. So I researched the vaudeville circuit at time and found Bessie Smith in theatre. She was a blues singer who sang in speakeasies; and I learned about the 20s and 30s through her eyes. On day of the exam, I came in singing, staying in character. He asked questions and I answered based on what Bessie Smith would have said.

Notice how rigorous the assessment was. She had to demonstrate far more understanding than simply answering a question, and this can be done by asking her to video her performance for your review, and that of her peers.

Other Sample Performances

Oral Presentations
Reader's Theatre
Exhibitions
Essays
Multimedia Presentations
Debates
Role-Playing
Experiments

Now, let's look at three additional samples of rigorous performances, one for each grade range. First, here's a sample assessment for high school math. Compare this to a test that might ask students to evaluate a set of linear equations and interpret them. Which provides a more rigorous assessment?

Sample High School Mathematics Performance Tasks

PARCC High School Task: Golf Balls in Water

Part A: Students analyze data from an experiment involving the effect on the water level of adding golf balls to a glass of water in which they:

- ◆ Explore approximately linear relationships by identifying the average rate of change.
- ◆ Use a symbolic representation to model the relationship.

Part B: Students suggest modifications to the experiment to increase the rate of change.

Part C: Students interpret linear functions using both parameters by examining how results change when a glass with a smaller radius is used by:

- ◆ Explaining how the y-intercepts of two graphs will be different.
- ◆ Explaining how the rate of change differs between two experiments.
- ◆ Using a table, equation or other representation to justify how many golf balls should be used.

Herman, J. L., & Linn, R. L. (2013). On the road to assessing deeper learning: The status of Smarter Balanced and PARCC assessment consortia (C RESST Report No. 823). Los Angeles: University of California, National Center for Research on Evaluation, Standards, and Student Testing, as found in Hammond, *Next Generation Assessment: Moving Beyond the Bubble Test to Support 21st-Century Learning.*

Next, let's look at a middle school science example that can be easily adapted to a social studies task.

Middle School Science Example

Using their knowledge of past catastrophic events that have affected the Earth and life on Earth such as earthquakes, volcanic eruptions, weather devastations and asteroid contact, students must predict the next catastrophic event that is likely to occur. They must also support their prediction with a minimum of three sources other than the classroom text. The student will present this information in the form of a video-based presentation or by electronic submission in a form the entire class can review such as Blackboard or Canvas.

Finally, we turn our attention to an upper elementary art example.

Sample Elementary Art Example

Students view an electronic art gallery of work created by their classmates. Each student chooses one piece of art and writes a short critique. The critique must include the student's opinion of the artwork, support of the opinion based on the lesson taught by the teacher and the student's own experiences and recommendations for improvement.

Performance-based assessments can provide a deeper look at student learning. Additionally, in a remote learning setting, the likelihood of students searching for an answer online rather than completing their own work is slim. Although you may want some students to work individually, there may be times you prefer that students work in groups. I mentioned several tools earlier when discussing Four Corners, each of which works well with any group work. I also find shared Google Docs particularly useful.

Grading Practices

I've found that grading is one of the most controversial aspects of teaching, and it can be an immediate roadblock to increasing rigor. As one teacher recently said to me, "The only thing my students and their parents care about is an A. They don't want rigor if it means lower grades."

When I started teaching elementary and junior high school, evaluating students was a struggle. I was never sure if I was doing it correctly or if there was one correct way to evaluate and grade. Advice from colleagues was pretty simple: Be able to back up anything you put down as a grade, and save everything. I kept a file of student folders, which included every paper or test that was graded. I mainly used them if a parent or a student questioned a grade. As I look back on that experience, I see how focused I was on the wrong thing, particularly since those files were a treasure chest of information with far more potent uses.

During that period, I looked on grading as having to prove that my opinion (the grade) was correct. I felt as though I was on the defensive, and as a result, grading was my least favorite task. I wish I had read these principles then because they would have helped me understand how to use grades more effectively.

However, a different set of circumstances helped me. After I started teaching remedial students, grades mattered differently to my students. In fact, they didn't matter much at all, so I shifted my attention. I thought about why I graded something, how I graded it and, lastly, how I could explain it to my students and parents in a way that would help them see why learning was important. As a result, my evaluation of students and the grading process became more authentic and valuable to me and my students.

Grading Without Guilt

Out of my experiences, I've come to realize that although there is no perfect way to grade, there are steps we can take to minimize the negative aspects of grading.

Minimizing Negative Aspects of Grading

Recognize the value of grading to students, parents and others.

Shift the emphasis to learning.

Provide clear guidelines.

Require quality work.

Communicate clearly.

Be patient.

EAB (eab.com) is a company that partners with schools to improve learning. They describe five recommendations for grading in a remote learning classroom.

Grading Recommendations

Only grade student performance on standards most essential to course content.

Substitute performance tasks for traditional assessments.

Consider deploying a hybrid grading approach to motivate students while preserving maximum flexibility.

Provide remote feedback before grading student work.

Adapt existing grading policies to avoid starting from scratch.

Source: https://eab.com/insights/expert-insight/district-leadership/how-to-create-a-grading-and-assessment-policy-for-distance-learning/

The most important action you can take with regard to grading is to determine what you want to accomplish (your purpose) and how you want students to demonstrate they have met your purpose (product).

To make this more concrete, I asked Missy to describe her grading procedures. As a seventh-grade language arts teacher, she points out that criterion-based grading is a key tool.

> With grading, it is even more important to use criterion-based grading. If in an asynchronous environment, there is no way to distinguish between homework vs classwork grades, and the categories seem arbitrary. To communicate very clearly to parents and students, grading should be centered around the skills and knowledge you will be teaching. For example, I used to have homework worth 10%, classwork worth 20%, quizzes for 30% and tests/projects/essays as 40%, as this was mandated by my department. However, once we began distance learning, I was given the freedom to revise this, based on what worked best for my students. To communicate progress in various areas effectively, I chose to use the following grading categories in my 7th grade Language Arts classroom: Reading skills (comprehension, figurative analysis, research, vocabulary development) are worth 20%, Writing skills (6+1 Traits of writing, conventions, grammar) are 20% of the grade, Speaking, Listening, Viewing skills (analysis of non-print texts, Flipgrid responses, presentations, class discussions/seminars over Google Meet) for 20%, and Culminating Synthesis/Evaluation Assessments (alternative-based assessments, essays, projects, etc.) equal 40%. I've found that, under this system, all constituents can more readily identify a students' academic strengths and weaknesses.

A Final Note

Assessment has two purposes: It allows students to demonstrate learning, and it allows you to measure that learning. It's important to use a mix of formative and summative assessment. Additionally, summative assessment should continue to be rigorous, even in a remote learning setting. A final part of assessment is determining your grading procedures, which should be appropriate to remote learning.

Points to Ponder

Use the following sentence starters to reflect on the chapter.

♦ I learned . . .
♦ I'd like to try . . .
♦ I can adapt this strategy to my own remote teaching by . . .
♦ I need . . .
♦ I'd like to share something from this chapter with . . .

7

Challenges Related to Rigor and Remote Learning

As you incorporate rigor into remote learning, there are a variety of challenges you'll experience that go beyond academics. Let's look at three: motivating students, creating a positive climate and partnering with parents and families.

How Can I Motivate Students?

When I talk with teachers in my workshops, they regularly ask me, "My students don't really care about learning. What is going to happen when I raise the level of rigor?" As a part of increasing rigor in the classroom, we must activate student motivation. Sometimes we try to use extrinsic motivators, such as rewards or grades. They can help, but typically only with rote tasks, and they only last a short time. Intrinsic motivation comes from within a student and builds over time for a long-lasting impact. Students are more motivated when they value what they are doing and when they believe they have a chance for success. Those are the two keys: value and success. Do students see value in the lesson? Do they believe they can be successful?

Value

We typically think of value as the real-life relevance of learning. However, there are three ways students see value in learning.

```
Relevance
Activities
Relationship
```

First, relevance is important. Although many students see the relevance of technology, we must move beyond that. Ideally, your students will make their own connections about the relevance of content, and you should provide them opportunities to make those connections independently, which may occur based on an exploration of internet resources. But there are also times that you will need to facilitate that understanding. I observed a science teacher who was very effective in helping his students see value in lessons. At the beginning of the year, he asked his students to write about their goals for life after high school. During a lesson on chemical mixtures, he realized that Shaquandra was struggling. He asked her, "Why is an understanding of chemical mixtures important to you?" Puzzled, she replied, "I don't know. I don't think it is." He then guided her to a realization that since she wanted to own a beauty shop, she would need to know about mixtures when using chemical treatments on a customer's hair. Her motivation to participate in the lesson increased tremendously.

For younger students, relevance may look a bit different. For example, one day my niece called me. Jenna was quite excited about being in second grade. In math, the teacher provided math word problems, and one included the name of Jenna's dog. For her, that was a connection to her life.

However, there are times when we are teaching something that, frankly, really doesn't have any relevance to our students. When I was a teacher, I remember some concepts that I taught only because they were tested at the end of the year. In that case, we need to turn to another option.

The second way students see value is through activities. Students are more motivated when they are actively engaged in learning. It's important for us to weave purposeful, engaging activities for all students throughout our instruction. Video presentations are important, but you may want to do small groups rather than large groups. My webinars regularly include activities to complete prior to our session, open-ended and closed-ended chat responses, polls and follow-up activities. My goal is for teachers to be involved throughout the webinar, which strengthens their learning.

Finally, students see value through their relationship with you. No matter their age, students want you to like them. They want to know you care. If you have a positive relationship with your students, they will do their absolute best for you. And if you have a negative relationship with a student, he or she will typically withdraw or act out, and he or she will likely not learn as much. Building a relationship remotely presents unique challenges and requires teachers to adjust how to connect with students. Strategies to consider are creating a personal profile for yourself and students—a "virtual show and tell" that can be regularly updated, scheduling video time with a small group of students for a "morning meeting" or advisory time, or sending electronic messages. One of the easiest ways to connect is to share stories about yourself, whether during a video presentation or in writing.

Another alternative when you are presenting via video is to use a background that contains something personal. I recently watched a guest on a news show who was appearing via video. He had a painting on his wall that was in the background that showed a scene from North Carolina. Because I am from that state, I felt an immediate connection.

During a recent webinar, my kitten jumped up in front of my computer. I was embarrassed, but the group thought it was funny. They immediately posted comments in the chats about their own animals. For them, it made me more "real." The same is true for you. You'll want to make sure anything personal is appropriate and is not distracting, but it is a way to build a shared relationship.

Success

Success is the second key to student motivation. Students are more motivated when they feel like they are successful or that they have a chance to be successful. If Dustin thinks an assignment is too hard and that he must complete it on his own, he is likely to give up. But if he is given a challenge, as well as assurances from you that you will be there, even from a distance, to guide and support him, he will put try to accomplish the task, and he will likely succeed.

Success is a particular challenge with remote learning. Students who normally struggle even with you providing on-site help are particularly susceptible to failure in a remote setting. Strategies such as providing step-by-step instructions and frequent check-ins are critical. There are a variety of instructional techniques to help students be successful, and we discussed several examples in Chapter 4. When increasing rigor effectively, teachers thoroughly integrate a focus on success in their classrooms, and this is even more important with remote learning.

How Can I Create a Positive Climate in a Remote Setting?

There is much information available on classroom climate, but little on climate in a remote learning setting. I think of climate as the strategies a teacher uses to create the opportunity for his or her students to thrive. As I wrote this section and reflected on my teaching, including my technology-based instruction, I realized that climate can also be described as a series of statements. As the author of several A–Z books, here are my statements that reflect what I believe should be a part of a remote learning climate.

A Positive Remote Learning Climate

Allow students opportunities just to talk to you.
Build routines to provide predictability for students.
Choices, when appropriate, give students a sense of control.
Details and clarity help students learn.

Enthusiasm from you builds student excitement.

Facilitate independence; don't solve all problems for students.

Growth is important; track it.

Hello! Check in personally with students as often as possible.

Identify each student's strengths and build on them.

Join with other teachers to provide creative classroom opportunities.

Kindness counts—no bullying!

Listening is harder to do remotely, but it's more important.

Move close to the camera during a video to be close to your students.

Never give up—on yourself or your students.

Ownership still matters—create opportunities for students to feel a part of the classroom.

Pacing of work is important; build in application and reflection.

Quality is more important than quantity.

Raise expectations, but make sure students know they can always get help.

Smile, Smile, Smile.

Take your time (don't go too fast when talking to students).

Understand that students have distractions at home.

Value the aspects of remote learning, even if you miss traditional school.

We are all in this together. Group learning is especially important with remote instruction.

X-factor—technology problems can be an obstacle. Plan for it.

You make a difference every day even when it doesn't feel like it.

Zero in on learning, not the technology.

How Can I Work With Parents and Families?

Partnering with the parents and families of your students provides advantages to you, your students and their families. Families will have a better idea of what's happening in school, which also allows them to help support their son or daughter at home. Students benefit when they receive encouragement at home. And teachers benefit when learning is reinforced and supported by parents and families.

Communicating and working with parents and families is a particular challenge in a remote learning setting. It's still our responsibility to connect with parents, and the benefits outweigh any costs in terms of time. There are three ways to partner with parents.

> Connect
> Inform
> Encourage

Connect

Many parent and family partnerships are destroyed before they start because the teacher believes it is someone else's responsibility to prompt a connection. This was exactly the attitude of my former colleague, who told me, "If a parent doesn't contact you, that is great. Just lay low and you'll be able to do what you want." If you believe it's the responsibility of parents and families to communicate and/or follow-up with you, that attitude comes through when you talk with them. Connecting with parents is not an extra job; it is part of your job. There is no way you can truly help your students be successful without the support of their parents.

Connecting With Parents

Learn their names.
Always begin with a positive comment.
Avoid blame.
Share good news regularly.
Ask them to help you understand their son or daughter.
Ask for input with selected decisions.
Hold virtual open houses.
Hold virtual teacher conferences.

One particular activity I like is a vision letter. Ideally completed at the start of the year, you ask parents and family members to write you a letter. In the letter, they imagine it is the end of the school year, and it was the best school year ever for their child, grandchild, niece, nephew, etc. They look "back" on the year and describe for you what happened. What did they think went well, what did the student learn or why did their student thrive? They are able to be as detailed as they would like and can write the letter, provide a video or use any format they prefer. When you read the letter, you may be surprised at what you learn. I've found families have never been asked their point of view on what would make a successful school year, and they are happy to share. In many cases, I've heard parents share how honored they were that a teacher would want to know what they think.

Missy Miles likes to connect with parents while students are also present.

> It is beneficial to connect with a parent and child in a live Zoom meeting or Google Meet. Seeing them face to face allows the personal side of you to connect. You can also talk more freely, without possible miscommunication of tone. Students can ask questions in front of parents and you can clarify, with the parent hearing, how you help his/her child through the problem without giving the answer or solution. These meetings also make it possible to share your screen and literally walk them through how to find information or vice versa: the students can share the screen, which allows you to walk him/her their work with coaching and guidance. Parents are typically very appreciative of the "meeting" face to face as they are experiencing a new role for which they have not been trained.

Inform

Next, keep your students' parents and families informed. Too often, problems occur when there is a misunderstanding. You'll want to communicate detailed information at the start of the year, then provide ongoing material throughout the year. How much? That depends on your situation, the parents and families and your students. However, one parent I spoke with said, "Teachers shouldn't feel pressure to communicate with me everyday. 2–3 times per week is enough." Again, the frequency really depends on the needs of your students, which includes their age, but I'd recommend a minimum of once a week to keep everyone focused.

What types of information should you share? That is typically determined by what you want to accomplish. Some parents need more detailed information; others need very little. As I talked with parents who were adjusting to the new "remote reality" due to COVID-19, they shared a variety of comments.

Parents' Comments

I'd like to know how to prioritize if we don't have time to do everything.

What is the best way for me to help my child?

How do I know I am doing the right things?

How will I know if my son or daughter is successful?

As you read their comments, you are probably thinking about information you should provide. One of the goals of parent communication is to provide details about the most critical aspects of remote learning.

General Tips for Parents

Encourage your son or daughter to give 100% at all times, but understand when the stress is simply too much for him or her and it's time for a break.

Reinforce concepts and habits the teacher is trying to build. If Miguel is learning how to multiply percentages, have him help you calculate the sales tax of a grocery or online order.

If possible, create a designated, quiet, well-lit environment at home with all of the materials necessary for completing school tasks (extra paper, scissors, pens, pencils, pencil sharpener, a dictionary, markers, highlighters, a ruler, calculator, index cards, etc.).

Prevent brain freeze—allow your son or daughter to take a short break every 30 minutes or between tasks. Taking time to move around during that break is beneficial.

Be careful not to give answers; instead, offer advice about where to look for an answer.

Follow the schedule and guidelines provided by the teacher. If you need to, ask the teacher for help prioritizing tasks for your son or daughter.

In addition to providing general tips for parents, you might consider creating information sheets about key topics related to your specific content.

Sample Topical Tips

Problem-Solving in Math

How to Read Online

Searching for Information Online

Participating in Zoom (or other appropriate technology tools)

Here's an example of a topical tip sheet on rigor that helps parents understand how to support increased rigor for their children.

Rigor Tip Sheet for Parents

Rigor is having high expectations for your son or daughter, providing appropriate help when they need it and giving them the chance to show you what they have learned in a way that demonstrates higher-order thinking.

1. Rigor is being challenged on grade level, but support is provided, like reading guides, to help students navigate through difficult or unfamiliar text.

2. Rigor is helping your son or daughter think for himself or herself. You can help your son or daughter do this teaching him or her to think beyond the text by asking questions starting with "What if . . ."

3. Rigor is helping your son or daughter make connections among the disciplines. Ask, "How does this topic relate to what you are studying in your other classes?"

4. Rigor is allowing your son or daughter to explore and discover. It is okay if he or she takes a while to get the answer and you can see it clearly. Home is the appropriate place for your son or daughter to take their time and process while solving problems.

5. Rigor is providing guidance, not answers. When your son or daughter asks for help, provide guidance, not answers. Too much help teaches that someone will do the work for him or her.

6. Rigor is providing a supportive environment at home for your son or daughter to work. He or she needs to know it is okay if his or her answers are not perfect and that he or she can ask for help as long as he or she has exhausted other measures such as checking class notes, looking to the text or other reading material, or doing some light research online.

7. Rigor is using and teaching your son or daughter to use positive language when confronted with a challenge. "I can't" is not a phrase anyone may use in your home. Instead, say, "I am having trouble getting this done. I am going to try to do it by myself, but I may need some help."

8. Rigor is having high expectations for your son or daughter and cheering them on when they are frustrated or challenged.

Information About Developmental Needs

In addition to providing standard information to parents and families, they need information and assistance regarding the developmental needs of their children. I asked Missy if the families of her students had this issue and, if so, how she recommends teachers address this.

> Parents oftentimes see their child in a different light during remote learning: as student. This realization is surprising to some, as I had many parents tell me they had no idea their son/daughter had such a hard time putting thoughts to paper or following written directions. While this comes to no surprise to you as teacher, they may have never seen this side of their child. Coaching them through developmental needs will help tremendously. You may need to remind them that it is normal to some degree, or you may have to explain how you help their child through those difficulties in the classroom.

Encourage

Encouraging parents and families is also a critical part of building a relationship, and it is especially important during remote learning.

I called every parent during the first month of school to introduce myself and tell them something positive about their son or daughter. I thought of parent relationships like a bank; I needed to make a deposit before I made a withdrawal. I didn't want my first phone call to be the one about a poor grade or a discipline problem. One time it took 17 calls to reach a parent before I was finally successful. It took about five minutes to convince her I wasn't calling because Marcus was in trouble. She finally said she had never received a call from a teacher telling her something positive about her son. She thanked me and immediately offered her help anytime I needed it. Five weeks later when Marcus struggled behaviorally, she supported me 100%.

Most of the parents I spoke with said they needed even more encouragement during remote learning. See if you have heard any of these comments.

Parents' Comments

How do I get started?

I'm not sure if I'm doing the right things.

I am overwhelmed! I don't know what to do next.

How do I know what is most important?

Providing information responds to some concerns, but just as students need encouragement, so do their parents and families. Some parents are working at home and trying to help their sons and daughters; some are working and cannot help until the workday ends; some have multiple children and are just overwhelmed. And, just like students, some need more encouragement than others. As you build relationships and communicate regularly, you will know when and how to encourage parents and families. Much of your encouragement will be comments that praise what they are doing well, as well as sharing suggestions in a supportive manner. Your words and any nonverbal cues will make a difference to them.

Formats for Encouraging Families

Video Message

Email

Chat

Snail Mail

Phone Call

You can also encourage parents and family with public recognition.

Publicly Recognizing Parents and Families

"Shout-outs" on Social Media (follow appropriate privacy
   guidelines)

Highlight an Example From the Family Through Classroom
   Communication

Send a Message to Your Student Praising His or Her Parent
   or Family

A Final Note

As a part of planning and incorporating rigor in your classroom, there are key issues to address. When you pay attention to student motivation, the virtual classroom climate and partnering with parents and families, your students are more likely to succeed.

Points to Ponder

Use the following sentence starters to reflect on the chapter.

- ◆ I learned . . .
- ◆ I'd like to try . . .
- ◆ I can adapt this strategy to my own remote teaching by . . .
- ◆ I need . . .
- ◆ I'd like to share something from this chapter with . . .

8

Continue the Conversation

As you have read the various strategies throughout the book, I hope you have found ideas you can incorporate in your teaching. However, consideration of ideas should only be the first step. Application of material is the ultimate goal, just as it is with your students. Here are three ways you can apply what you have learned.

Create an Action Plan for Your Classroom
Work With Other Teachers in Your School and District
Share What You Are Doing

Create an Action Plan for Your Classroom

First, revisit your thoughts from the *Points to Ponder* in each chapter. Then, using that information, create a plan for your classroom.

Idea from Book/Chapter	Ways You Will Use/ Adapt the Idea	When You Will Use the Idea (specific lesson, topic, or unit)

Work With Other Teachers in Your School and District

Next, work with other teachers in your school and/or district to collaboratively implement ideas from the book. One strategy, lesson studies, can be effective.

Lesson studies emphasize working in small groups to plan, teach, observe and critique a lesson. It's an excellent reflection of the principles of professional learning communities, as the goal is to systematically examine your teaching in order to become more effective.

In a lesson study, teachers work together to develop a detailed plan for a lesson. One member of the group teaches the lesson to his or her students, while other members of the group observe. Next, the group discusses their observations about the lesson and student learning.

Teachers revise the lesson based on their observations, then a second group member teaches the lesson, with other members once again observing. Then, the group meets to discuss the revised lesson. Finally, teachers talk about what the study lesson taught them and how they can apply the learning in their own classroom.

Let's apply this to the remote learning classroom. After working together to develop the detailed plan, a member teaches the group virtually. If it is a synchronous lesson, perhaps teachers can attend to observe. If it is a recorded video, teachers can observe at their convenience. If it is a lesson in which students work independently to complete a task, other teachers review how the lesson is presented, as well as students' responses. From there, you follow the process, just virtually with the adaptations. One caution—be sure you are addressing any student privacy issues.

Lesson studies allow teachers to collaboratively refine the implementation of strategies so that you can all improve your remote teaching.

Share What You Are Doing

Finally, share what you are doing within and outside your district. Explain your efforts to your administrators, other schools within your district, your district leaders and the school board.

I find it particularly helpful to share your successes with your school board. That isn't something many teachers think about, but it allows you to showcase your work and possibly build a case for additional resources. There are several tips for communicating with your school board, all of which can occur at virtual board meetings.

- ◆ Identify a parent or community spokesperson to help deliver your message to the board.
- ◆ Frame the importance of your issue in your opening statement. Link it to board goals and how students will be successful once they leave your school.
- ◆ Describe your plan in such a way that the board can see the link between your overall school improvement efforts and their goals.
- ◆ Share examples of your work to illustrate the impact. It can be very helpful to highlight the effect of greater rigor on one or more students.
- ◆ Give recognition to the individuals who have contributed to your success. It is a time for you to be modest and allow others to be recognized.
- ◆ Conclude your presentation by aligning your vision with the board's vision for the district.

Next, share what you are doing with the larger professional community of educators. We are all learners, and I find teachers are eager to hear what other teachers are doing. You can share ideas and screen shots via Twitter (be sure to tag me @barbblackburn), Facebook (Barbara Blackburn), Instagram or any other social media outlets. You might also consider writing an article for a state journal or an online outlet such as MiddleWeb or EdCircuit. There are also a variety of blogs that share teachers' ideas.

Finally, on a personal note, thank you for investing your time in my book. I strive to provide practical information you can immediately apply with your students. The best compliment I receive is from a teacher who has used or adapted these techniques in his or her classroom. When that happens, it means I have made a difference, which is hopefully something I have done for you. I always like hearing from you, whether you are sharing what you have done or asking me a question. Please feel free to reach out to me via my website, www.barbarablack burnonline.com. I'd like to leave you with a thought a teacher shared with me. On your worst day, on the day that everything has gone wrong—the technology didn't work, your own children were asking you questions while you were also trying to answer your students' questions, you were trying unsuccessfully to reach certain parents—on that day, you are someone's best hope. In fact, I would tell you on that day, you are not someone's best hope. You are their only hope. You make a difference, even when you don't feel like it. You really make a difference, especially when you don't feel like it. Thank you for all you do for your students.

Bibliography

54 Different examples of formative assessment. (n.d.). Retrieved from http://cmrweb.gfps.k12.mt.us/uploads/2/7/3/6/27366965/formative_assessment_ppt.pdf

The Academy of Inquiry Based Learning. (n.d.). *Supporting instructors, empowering students, transforming mathematics learning.* Retrieved from www.inquirybasedlearning.org

Almarode, J., Fisher, D., Frey, N., & Hattie, J. (2018). *Visible learning for science.* Thousand Oaks, CA: Corwin.

Ames, R., & Ames, C. (1990). Motivation and effective teaching. In B. F. Jones & L. Idol (Eds.), *Dimensions of thinking and cognitive instruction.* Hillsdale, NJ: Erlbaum.

Barrell, J. (2007). *Problem-based learning: An inquiry approach* (2nd ed.). Thousand Oaks, CA: Corwin Press.

Bellanca, J. (2010). *Enriched learning projects: A practical pathway to 21st century skills.* Bloomington, IN: Solution Tree, Inc.

Benjamin, A. (2008). *Formative assessment for English language arts.* New York, NY: Routledge.

Berger, M. *How to create a grading and assessment policy for distance learning.* Retrieved April 12, 2020, from https://eab.com/insights/expert-insight/district-leadership/how-to-create-a-grading-and-assessment-policy-for-distance-learning/

Black, P., Harrison, C., Lee, C., Marshall, B., & William, D. (2004). Working inside the black box: Assessment for learning in the classroom. *Phi Delta Kappan, 86,* 9–21.

Blackburn, B. R. (2008). Literacy from A to Z: *Engaging students in reading, writing, speaking, & listening.* New York, NY: Routledge.

Blackburn, B. R. (2012). *Rigor made easy.* New York, NY: Routledge.

Blackburn, B. R. (2014). *Rigor in your classroom: A toolkit for teachers.* New York, NY: Routledge.

Blackburn, B. R. (2016a). *Classroom instruction from A to Z: How to promote student learning* (2nd ed.). New York, NY: Routledge.

Blackburn, B. R. (2016b). *Motivating struggling learners: Ten strategies for student success*. New York, NY: Routledge.

Blackburn, B. R. (2017). *Rigor and assessment in the classroom*. New York, NY: Routledge.

Blackburn, B. R. (2018). *Rigor is not a four-letter word* (3rd ed.). New York, NY: Routledge.

Blackburn, B. R. (2019). *Rigor and differentiation in the classroom*. New York, NY: Routledge.

Blackburn, B. R., & Armstrong, A. (2019). *Rigor in the 6–12 math and science classroom*. New York, NY: Routledge.

Blackburn, B. R., & Armstrong, A. (2020). *Rigor in the K-5 math and science classroom*. New York, NY: Routledge.

Blackburn, B. R., Armstrong, A., & Miles, M. (2018). Using writing to spark learning in math, science, and social studies. *ASCD Express*, *13*(16). Retrieved from www.ascd.org/ascd-express/vol13/1316-blackburn.aspx?utm_source=ascdexpress&utm_medium=email&utm_campaign=Express%2D13%2D16

Blackburn, B. R., & Miles, M. (2019). *Rigor in the 6–12 language arts and social studies classroom*. New York, NY: Routledge.

Blackburn, B. R., & Miles, M. (2020). *Rigor in the K-5 language arts and social studies classroom*. New York, NY: Routledge.

Blackburn, B. R., & Witzel, B. (2013). *Rigor for students with special needs*. New York, NY: Routledge.

Blackburn, B. R., & Witzel, B. (2018). *Rigor in the RTI/MTSS classroom*. New York, NY: Routledge.

Bondie, R. (2020, April 23). Practical tips for teaching online small-group discussions. *Association for Supervision and Curriculum Development*, *15*(16).

Christopher, D. (2015). *The successful virtual classroom: How to design and facilitate interactive and engaging live online learning*. New York: American Management Association.

Clark, H., & Avrith, T. (2017). *The google infused classroom: A guidebook to making thinking visible and amplifying student voice*. Del Mar, CA: Elevate Books Edu.

Class Tech Tips. (n.d.). About Monica—Class tech tips. *Class Tech Tips*. Retrieved July 20, 2018, from https://classtechtips.com/about-monica/

Clayton, H. *The art of questioning: The student's role.* Retrieved April 25, 2020, from https://justaskpublications.com/just-ask-re source-center/e-newsletters/msca/the-art-of-questioning-the-student-role/

Cleary, J. A., Morgan, T. A., & Marzano, R. J. (2018). *Classroom techniques for creating conditions for rigorous instruction.* West Palm Beach, FL: Learning Sciences International.

Coiro, J., Dobler, E., & Pelekis, K. (2019). *From curiosity to deep learning: Personal digital inquiry in grades K-5.* Portsmouth, NH: Stenhouse Publishers.

Cooper, J. M. (2006). *Classroom teaching skills.* Boston, MA: Cengage.

Curwin, R. L. (2010). *Meeting students where they live: Motivation in urban schools.* Alexandria, VA: Association of Supervision and Curriculum Development.

Daniels, H., Zemelman, S., & Steineke, N. (2007). *Content-area writing: Every teacher's guide.* Portsmouth, NH: Heinemann.

The DBQ Project. (2018, July 19). The DBQ project. *The DBQ Project.* Retrieved July 20, 2018, from www.dbqproject.com/

Edmondson, E. (2012, March). Wiki literature circles: Creating digital learning communities. *The English Journal, 101*(4), 43–49. National Council of Teachers of English.

Eisenbach, B. B., & Greathouse, P. (2018). *The online classroom: Resources for effective middle level virtual education.* Association for Middle Level Education. Charlotte, NC: Information Age Publishing.

Ferriter, W. M., & Garry, A. (2010). *Teaching the iGeneration: 5 easy ways to introduce essential skills with web 2.0 tools.* Bloomington, IN: Solution Tree Press.

Fielding, L., & Roller, C. (1992, May). Making difficult books accessible and easy books acceptable. *The Reading Teacher,* 678–685.

Fisher, D., & Frey, N. (n.d.). *Scaffolds for learning: The key to guided instruction.* Retrieved June 20, 2017, from www.ascd.org/publications/books/111017/chapters/Scaffolds-for-Learning@-The-Key-to-Guided-Instruction.aspx

Fisher, D., Frey, N., & Lapp, D. (2012a). *Teaching students to read like detectives.* Bloomington, IN: Solution Tree Press.

Fisher, D., Frey, N., & Lapp, D. (2012b). *Text complexity: Raising rigor in reading.* Newark, DE: International Reading Association.

Fraser, C. (2018). *Love the questions: Reclaiming research with curiosity and passion.* Portsmouth, NH: Stenhouse Publishing.

Gerstein, J. (2019). *Learning in the making: How to plan, execute, and assess powerful makerspace lessons.* Alexandria, VA: Association of Supervision and Curriculum Development.

Guskey, T. R., & Bailey, J. M. (2001). *Developing grading and reporting systems for student learning.* Thousand Oaks, CA: Corwin Press.

Hattie, J., & Yates, G. (2008). *Visible learning: A synthesis of over 800 meta-analyses relating to achievement.* New York, NY: Routledge Taylor & Francis Group.

Hattie, J., & Yates, G. (2014). *Visible learning and the science of how we learn.* New York, NY: Routledge Taylor & Francis Group.

Heick, T. *A guide to questioning in the classroom.* Retrieved April 12, 2020, from www.teachthought.com/critical-thinking/quick-guide-questioning-classroom/

Highfill, L., Hilton, K., & Landis, S. (2016). *The hyperdoc handbook: Digital lesson design using google apps.* Del Mar, CA: Elevate Books Edu.

Jansen, A. (2020). *Rough draft math: Revising to learn.* Portsmouth, NH: Stenhouse Publishers.

Keeler, A., & Miller, L. (2016). *50 things to go further with google classroom: A student-centered approach.* San Diego, CA: Dave Burgess Consulting, Inc.

Lapp, D. (2016). *Turning the page on complex texts: Differentiated scaffolds for close reading instruction.* Bloomington, IN: Solution Tree Press.

Maiers, A., & Sandvold, A. (2011). *The passion-driven classroom: A framework for teaching and learning.* New York, NY: Routledge.

Marzano, R. J. (2007). *The art of science and teaching: A comprehensive framework for effective instruction.* Alexandria, VA: Association for Supervision and Curriculum Development.

Marzano, R. J. (2010). Giving students meaningful work. *Educational Leadership, 68,* 82–84.

Marzano, R. J. (2012). Art and science of teaching: The many uses of exit slips. *Educational Leadership, 70*(2), 80–81.

Marzano, R. J., Pickering, D. J., & Heflebower, T. (2011). *The highly engaged classroom*. Bloomington, IN: Marzano Resources.

Marzano, R. J., Pickering, D. J., & Pollock, J. E. (2001). *Classroom instruction that works: Research-based strategies for increasing student achievement*. Alexandria, VA: Association for Supervision and Curriculum Development.

McTighe, J., Doubet, K. J., & Carbaugh, E. M. (2020). *Designing authentic performance tasks and projects*. Alexandria, VA: Association of Supervision and Curriculum Development.

McTighe, J., & Silver, H. F. (2020). *Teaching for deeper learning: Tools to engage students in meaning making*. Alexandria, VA: Association for Supervision and Curriculum Development.

McTighe, J., & Wiggins, G. (2013). *Essential questions: Opening doors to student understanding*. Alexandria, VA: Association for Supervision and Curriculum Development.

Merrill, J., & Merrill, K. (2019). *The interactive class: Using technology to make learning more relevant and engaging in the elementary classroom*. Del Mar, CA: Elevate Books Edu.

Miller, A. *Formative assessment in distance learning*. Retrieved April 12, 2020, from www.edutopia.org/article/formative-assessment-distance-learning

Miller, A. *Summative assessment in distance learning*. Retrieved April 12, 2020, from www.edutopia.org/article/summative-assessment-distance-learning

Morgan, N., & Saxton, J. (2006). *Asking better questions* (2nd ed.). Ontario, Canada: Pembroke Publishers.

O'Conner, K. (2002). *How to grade for learning: Linking grades to standards*. Thousand Oaks, CA: Corwin Press.

Pitler, H., Hubbell, E. R., & Kuhn, M. (2012). *Using technology with classroom instruction that works* (2nd ed.). Alexandria, VA: Association for Supervision and Curriculum Development.

Popham, W. J. (2008). *Transformative assessment*. Alexandria, VA: Association for Supervision and Curriculum Development.

Reason, C., Reason, L., & Guiler, C. (2017). *Creating the anywhere, anytime classroom: A blueprint for learning online in grades K-12*. Bloomington, IN: Solution Tree Press.

Regier, N. (2012). *Book two: Formative assessment strategies.* Regier Educational Resources. Retrieved May 21, 2018, from www.stma.k12.mn.us/documents/DW/Q_Comp/Formative AssessStrategies.pdf

Richardson, W. (2010). *Blogs, wikis, podcasts, and other powerful web tools for classrooms* (3rd ed.). Thousand Oaks, CA: Corwin Press.

Rothstein, D., & Santana, L. (2011). *Make just one change: Teach students to ask their own questions.* Cambridge, MA: Harvard Education Press.

Sample Exit Tickets. (n.d.). Retrieved from http://science-class.net/Assessment/Exit-tickets/exit_tickets.htm

Sangiovanni, J. J., Katt, S., & Dykema, K. J. (2020). *Productive math struggle: A 6-point action plan for fostering perseverance.* Thousand Oaks, CA: Corwin.

Santa, C., Havens, L., & Macumber, E. (1996). *Creating independence through student-owned strategies.* Dubuque, IA: Kendall Hunt.

Smith, G. E., & Throne, S. (2010). *Differentiating instruction with technology in K-5 classrooms.* Eugene, OR: International Society for Technology Integration.

Southern Regional Education Board. (2004). *Ten strategies for creating a classroom culture of high expectations.* Atlanta, Georgia: Author. Retrieved from http://publications.sreb.org/2004/04v03_Ten_Strategies.pdf

Stanley, T. (2014). *Performance-based assessment for the 21st century classroom.* Waco, TX: Prufrock Press.

Sun, Y. (2020). *Questioning techniques to engage students in critical thinking.* Retrieved April 16, 2020, from http://blog.tesol.org/questioning-techniques-to-engage-students-in-critical-thinking/

Tovani, C. (2011). *So what do they really know? Assessment that informs teaching and learning.* Portland, ME: Stenhouse.

Walsh, J. A., & Sattes, B. D. (2015). *Questioning for classroom discussion.* Alexandria, VA: Association for Supervision and Curriculum Development.

Wiggins, G., & McTighe, J. (2005). *Understanding by design, expanded* (2nd ed.). Alexandria, VA: Association for Supervision and Curriculum Development.

Williamson, R. (2012). *Research into Practice: Importance of high expectations*. Oregon Gear Up. Retrieved July 12, 2018, from https://oregongearup.org/sites/oregongearup.org/files/research-briefs/highexpectations.pdf

Willis, J., & Willis, M. (2020). *Research-based strategies to ignite student learning*. Alexandria, VA: Association for Supervision and Curriculum Development.

Wilson, D., & Conyers, M. (2016). *Teaching students to drive their brains*. Alexandria, VA: Association of Supervision and Curriculum Development.

Made in the USA
Middletown, DE
21 March 2023

27280755R00076